Never a Matter
of Indifference

DATE DUE

JUL 1 5 2004		
DEC 0 8 2004		
DEC 1 2004		
JAN 2 2005		
JAN 2 2005		
JAN 2 2005 FEB 0 8 2005		

Demco

This book is a publication
of the Hoover Institution's

Initiative on
American Individualism
and Values

The Hoover Institution
gratefully acknowledges

TAD AND DIANNE TAUBE

TAUBE FAMILY FOUNDATION

for their generous support
of this book project.

Never a Matter of Indifference

Sustaining Virtue in a Free Republic

EDITED BY

Peter Berkowitz

HOOVER INSTITUTION PRESS
Stanford University   Stanford, California

The Hoover Institution on War, Revolution and Peace,
founded at Stanford University in 1919 by Herbert Hoover,
who went on to become the thirty-first president of
the United States, is an interdisciplinary research center
for advanced study on domestic and international affairs.
The views expressed in its publications are entirely those of
the authors and do not necessarily reflect the views of the staff,
officers, or Board of Overseers of the Hoover Institution.

www.hoover.org

Hoover Institution Press Publication No. 520

First printing 2003
09   08   07   06   05   04   03   9   8   7   6   5   4   3   2   1

Manufactured in the United States of America

The paper used in this publication meets the minimum requirements
of American National Standard for Information Sciences—Permanence
of Paper for Printed Library Materials, ANSI Z39.48-1984. ♾

ISBN 0-8179-3962-8
Library of Congress Control No. 2003111853

The cultivation of all the personal, social, and benevolent virtues;—these never can be a matter of indifference in any well ordered community.

—Joseph Story, *Commentaries on the Constitution* (1833)

Contents

Acknowledgments

This book is the first fruit of the Hoover Institution's Initiative on American Individualism and Values. I wish to thank John Raisian, director of the Hoover Institution, and David Brady, director of research at the Hoover Institution, for their enthusiasm. Thanks also to David Davenport, my colleague in the initiative, for friendly collaboration. And we are all grateful to Tad Taube, whose generous support made this book possible.

Peter Berkowitz
Washington, D.C., 2003

Introduction

PETER BERKOWITZ

The contributors to this volume share a belief, an anxiety, and an aim. The belief is that public policy, both directly and indirectly, shapes the virtues citizens practice and the values citizens hold dear. The anxiety is that over the course of several decades, public policy in the United States has weakened the institutions of civil society, which play a crucial role in forming and sustaining the qualities of mind and character crucial to democratic self-government. The aim is to shed light on what can be done, consistent with the principles of a free society, to establish a more salutary relation between public policy and character.

The contributors form a diverse lot. Each works from a distinctive disciplinary and philosophical perspective. And each author addresses a discrete area of public policy. Certainly no individual author agrees with every observation and every assertion in every chapter. Some authors prefer to focus on virtue, or moral, political, and intellectual excellence. Others concentrate on values, or beliefs about what is proper, just, and good. In one way or another, all are critical of the regnant form of liberalism in America. At the same time, the authors are united in believing that the defense of liberty in our day requires a rethinking of the complex relation between citizens' character, civil society, and government.

This book is divided into two parts. Part I provides a theoretical overview, examining the teachings of America's founding liberalism about liberty and virtue, then exploring transformations of American liberalism catalyzed by the cultural upheavals of the 1960s. Part II explores the effect of post-1960s public policy on civic associations, on schooling, and on marriage and the family as well as the effect these transformed institutions have on our virtues and our values. Implicit in the overall organization of the book, and developed in one way or another in each chapter is the conviction that a more refined understanding of our liberalism— where it came from, how it has changed, and what belongs to its core and what in it is contingent and variable—puts us in a better position to reform public policy in a manner that serves the interests of individual freedom.

In the opening chapter, "Liberty and Virtue in the American Founding," Harvey Mansfield, a student of the history of political philosophy, puts the problem in plain terms: Liberty and virtue are in tension because liberty means doing what you want whereas virtue means doing what you ought. The achievement of the American founders, and of the philosophical authorities on which they relied, Mansfield shows, was their having reached an accommodation between liberty and virtue. John Locke paved the way in the *Second Treatise*, Mansfield approvingly observes, by means of a crucial equivocation. On the one hand, Locke argued that man's freedom is limited by God's authority. On the other hand, he maintained that by nature man's freedom knows only those limits that individuals give themselves. Neither of these propositions, in

Mansfield's view, reflects Locke's true position. Instead, Locke's teaching is contained in the determination to live with and gloss over the conflict between them. Then Montesquieu further paved the way to easing the tension between liberty and virtue by exposing the ill fit between the sternness and austerity of ancient virtue and the needs of a modern commercial republic.

According to Mansfield, the lesson drawn by America's founders, who studied both Locke and Montesquieu, was not that virtue must be abandoned, but rather that virtue must be reconceived in a way that made it suitable to the needs of liberty and commerce. In Benjamin Franklin's *Autobiography*, Mansfield finds a wry exposition of the new virtue: self-interested, pragmatic, industrious, focused on personal gain and private happiness. But is such virtue compatible with the needs of a free people who must govern themselves with a view to the public good? In the *Federalist*, Mansfield finds an approach that shows how it is. Taking individuals in a commercial republic as they are, Madison, Hamilton, and Jay set forth the principles of a political order that harnesses for the public good the energy of those whose ambitions find their satisfaction in politics. Through such devices as representation, the separation of powers, and checks and balances, their constitution arranges matters so that the private interest of ambitious men coincides with the advancement of the public's interest.

How stable is virtue that is grounded in self-interest, even when that self-interest is, as Mansfield argues it was by America's founders, well understood? Certainly no more stable than the beliefs, practices, and associations that foster it. In fact, the founders do not speak much about civil society, education, marriage, family, and religion. Critics have contended that this is because they embraced a crude, mechanical view of moral and political life, one that assumed that virtue, to the extent that it was necessary, would take care of itself. Based on their occasional remarks on the subject, however, it is more reasonable to conclude that their failure—if failure it was—was one of imagination. They recognized the connection between character and the institutions of civil society that sustain it, but they did not envision a political society in which the institutions of civil society, as a result of changes in culture and government, could no longer be counted on to discipline self-interest. In other words, what they did not prepare for were the challenges created by forces that culminated in the 1960s.

While acknowledging the breathtaking progress in civil rights witnessed in the 1960s, Stanley Kurtz focuses on the deleterious transformations that America's founding liberalism underwent in that decade of dazzling change. Offering a largely sociological interpretation, Kurtz argues that in the 1960s, liberalism, or the progressive liberalism that continues to dominate among our cultural elites, became a kind of secular religion—and in crucial respects, an illiberal religion. By religion, Kurtz means "an encompassing world-view that answers the big questions about life, dignifies our daily exertions with higher significance, and provides a rationale for meaningful collective action." The transformation of liberalism into a religion stemmed from liberalism's success. For as traditional religion declined, partly as a result of the quest for the personal freedom inspired by classical liberalism, many individuals sought ultimate meaning and nonnegotiable ideals in the mission to continuously expand the meaning of individual freedom and human equality. This infusion of holy significance into progressive liberalism, according to Kurtz, inclined the faithful to view those who opposed them—on abortion, affirmative action, feminism, the environment—as not merely mistaken but as enemies to be silenced, stigmatized, and routed from the field.

The tendency of liberalism to become a religion was anticipated in the nineteenth century, Kurtz points out, by the great French sociologist Emile Durkheim. Durkheim viewed the rise of the liberal doctrine of universal human rights with hope. He saw it as a new organizing principle that could take the place of tradi-tional religion in anchoring communal solidarities. But solidarity with those who suffer has proved too insubstantial a creed. And the inherent individualism of liberalism proved destabilizing. The "religion of rights," as Kurtz calls it, can undermine individual freedom by demanding unbending fidelity to a debatable political agenda. Instead of living with the tension between liberty and virtue as did America's founding liberalism, the left-liberalism that emerged from the 1960s suppresses virtue's claims in the name of freedom and equality.

The chapters in Part II are written in response to the short-comings of public policy over the last 30 years in dealing adequately with the distressing tendencies that Kurtz analyzes. But they also reflect the belief that America's founding liberalism continues to provide a standard for evaluating and correcting contemporary liberalism's excesses and unwise tendencies.

Focusing on recent political and legal history, and proceeding much in the spirit of Tocqueville's analysis of the role of associa-tions in nourishing democracy in America, David Davenport and Hanna Skandera examine civic associations and their impact on our virtues and values. Like Robert Putnam, who argued in the 1990s that the capacity of civic associations to produce social capital, or those "features of social organization such as networks, norms, and social trust that facilitate coordination and coopera-tion for mutual benefit,"[1] was on the decline, Davenport and Skan-dera see worrisome developments. They are particularly concerned about the changing relation between civic associations and gov-ernment. Increased federal funding of not-for-profit organiza-tions, especially in the 1960s as a result of President Johnson's Great Society programs, increased the dependence of civic asso-

---

1. Robert D. Putnam, "Bowling Alone: America's Declining Social Capital," *Journal of Democracy* 6, no. 1 (January 1995): 67.

ciations on government. Finding federal funding addictive, more and more civic associations were driven to change their agenda, moving in an explicitly political direction. This led them to become less a counterweight to than an arm of government. Moreover, in a series of important cases interpreting antidiscrimination law, the Supreme Court took steps to remove from civic associations control over decisions about their membership. According to Davenport and Skandera, these cases have had the unfortunate effect of undermining the capacity of civic associations to agree on values and foster virtues. Government action also has taken its toll on the independence and robustness of civic associations through onerous taxation, unfriendly property and zoning laws, and heavy regulation.

But Davenport and Skandera discern promising developments. From the first President Bush's vision of a "thousand points of light" through the Charitable Choice legislation that President Clinton signed into law as part of the 1996 welfare reform law to the second President Bush's faith-based initiative, Davenport and Skandera observe a growing understanding on the part of leaders in both parties that for government to reap the benefits of civic associations, it must find a way to preserve them in their independence, not to conscript them in the service of government.

In Chapter 4, Chester E. Finn Jr. argues that public school education in the United States faces a related paradox:

> Because we cherish freedom as a core value and insist that the state is the creature of its citizens, we are loath to allow state-run institutions to instruct tomorrow's citizens in how to think, how to conduct themselves, and what to believe. Because a free society is not self-maintaining, however, because its citizens must know something about democracy and individual rights and responsibilities, and because they must also learn how to behave in a law-abiding way that generally conforms to basic societal norms and values, it is the obligation of all educational

institutions, including primary and secondary schools, to assist
in the transmission of these core ideas, habits, and skills.

In Finn's view, however, public schools of late have done a poor
job in managing this paradox. Indeed, they increasingly have come
to have a positively ill influence on students' virtues and values by
teaching that virtues are fictitious, values are relative, democracy
is an arbitrary preference, and the aim of education is not the
acquisition of knowledge and the cultivation of the mind but the
promotion of self-expression and the enjoyment of self-esteem.

Reforming the public schools, Finn cautions, will be compli-
cated. For one thing, funding, and hence control, does not come
from a single source but from the federal, state, and local levels.
Although the federal government has expanded its role in the last
25 years in response to alarming studies that exposed the failure
of public high schools to teach their graduates the basics of reading
and writing, each level of government has retained a role in establishing the content of the curriculum. In addition, the reform
known as "character education" has proved, in Finn's estimation,
counterproductive. This is partly because most of what we call
character cannot be instilled through book learning. It is partly
because under the rubric of "social studies," public schools have
sought to teach a narrow left-liberal political activism as the sole
legitimate interpretation of our constitutional tradition. It is partly
because teachers, owing to their hypersensitivity to opinions that
do not conform precisely to today's dominant sensibility, have
purged from the curriculum many classic works that offer inval-
uable instruction about right and wrong, human tragedy and com-
edy, and the inexhaustible intricacies of the human heart. And it
is partly because educators have convinced themselves that the
purpose of education is to encourage students to develop their
own perspective on America rather than to learn what actually
happened in history and why America is worth respecting. Finn

finds hope in the school choice movement, not as an alternative to public schools but as a competitor and spur. Still, he reminds us, even in the best case, students spend a very limited portion of their lives in school, and therefore schools, public or private, cannot replace or compensate for—they can at best supplement—the education of character that takes place outside of school, particularly in the family.

Douglas Kmiec agrees that marriage and family are the foundation of education for liberty. Writing from a natural law perspective that is self-consciously religious and determinedly rational, Kmiec openly affirms that his position is "built on the paradox that we find individual freedom through obedience to our human natures." Today, marriage and the family, Kmiec argues, run contrary to our natures and thus are in a state of disarray. Divorce and illegitimacy rates remain high, single parenthood is common and on the upsurge, and family size continues to decline. Kmiec traces much of the problem to the predominate vision of marriage as a contract, flowing from the spirit of contemporary liberalism, in which spouses see themselves as individual partners cooperating for mutual advantage. By contrast, marriage as a mutual covenant, which Kmiec refers to as religious but which he insists is shown by reason to perfect our natures, envisages the "indissoluble completion of two otherwise incomplete individuals." In contemporary America, the individualist, or contractual, vision of marriage is reinforced in many ways: by the common teachings of school textbooks; by Supreme Court jurisprudence that insists upon strict separation of church and state; by state property laws that view spouses as individuals with distinct economic interests; by the propensity of women as well as men to elevate careers over family; by the routine reliance on day care; and by suburban communities that isolate families, both from neighbors and relatives.

Yet Kmiec is no pessimist. A free society gives individuals the opportunity to change social arrangements and alter the laws under which they live. Accordingly, Kmiec offers several proposals for strengthening marriage: revising "no-fault" divorce laws by requiring waiting periods and mediation; reviving the common law tort of "alienation of affections," which in cases of infidelity allows a spouse to sue his marriage partner's lover; ensuring in the event of divorce that caring for the children will be a top priority in the distribution of marital assets; providing more effective pre-marriage counseling concerning the rigors and rewards of marriage; and exploring means for restoring a proper balance between work and family. Kmiec is keenly aware that these reforms cut against the governing ethos of the age. He also is convinced that they would serve the best interests of individuals and of society. They would improve the prospects for spouses and parents to achieve lifelong happiness and for children to enjoy the stability and love in which the acquisition of basic virtues and the formation of sound values are rooted.

All political societies depend on the practice of virtue and the preservation of core values, but perhaps none more so than a liberal democracy, where equality in freedom enables individuals to live by their own lights and gives them large scope for making bad choices and indulging silly or false opinions. Threats to our virtues and values as well as to the beliefs, practices, and associations that sustain them come from many directions: popular culture, market excesses, foreign enemies. The contributors to this volume have tended to focus on the threats that come from a peculiar form of liberalism. Their warnings are animated by a common concern for freedom. And an optimism: So long as we enjoy the freedom of self-government, we have the opportunity to fortify the virtues and values that enable us to maintain ourselves as a free people.

PART I

THEORETICAL CONSIDERATIONS

ONE

Liberty and Virtue in the American Founding

HARVEY C. MANSFIELD

Liberty and virtue are not a likely pair. At first sight they seem to be contraries, for liberty appears to mean living as you please and virtue appears to mean living not as you please but as you ought. It doesn't seem likely that a society dedicated to liberty could make much of virtue, nor that one resolved to have virtue could pride itself on liberty. Yet liberty and virtue also seem necessary to each other. A free people, with greater opportunity to misbehave than a people in shackles, needs the guidance of an inner force to replace the lack of external restraint. And virtue cannot come from within, or truly be virtue, unless it is voluntary and people are free to choose it. Americans are, and think themselves to be, a free people first of all. Whatever virtue they have, and however much, is a counterpoint to the theme of liberty. But how do they manage to make virtue and liberty harmonious?

Locke and the American Founding

The answer is, in their founding. The American founding is an historical period that runs from the outbreak of the American Revolution in 1775 to the end of George Washington's presidency in 1801. This is a period of 25 years punctuated by two great events at which two great documents were produced, the Declaration of Independence in 1776 and the Constitution in 1787. America has a written founding, of which the Declaration of Independence provides the principle and the Constitution the formal structure. Behind the Declaration of Independence and the Constitution stands the political thought of John Locke, an Englishman who is America's philosopher. To Locke, or to Locke's contemporary audience, virtue seemed to be always in the company of religion; and favored by this association, virtue seemed to have the upper hand over liberty. Locke's task was to promote liberty, giving it priority over virtue, while not destroying virtue or denying religion. If he could accomplish this feat, his readers, first among them Americans, could frame a free constitution and found a free country in good conscience with the aid and comfort of God, or in the less pious words of the Declaration of Independence, "nature's god."

For Locke, then, the harmonizing of liberty and virtue begins from the harmonizing of liberty and religion. In the face of the apparent fact that the Christian religion tells men how to live, he must show, if he can, that it actually permits them to live in freedom. How does he proceed?

Locke gives two descriptions of the character of men in their fundamental relation to liberty. He says that they are the "workmanship" of God, that men are "his [God's] property" and so belong to God; but he also says that "every man has a property in his own person."[1] These appear to be directly contrary because the "workmanship argument" (as it is called by Locke's interpreters) would make man a slave of God[2] whereas the idea of property in one's own person sets him free to do with himself what he wishes. Thus Locke says, in accordance with the former, that men have no right to commit suicide ("everyone is bound . . . not to quit his Station wilfully"[3]). But in accordance with the latter, though saying nothing directly about a right of suicide, he pronounces that in the state of nature, man is "absolute lord of his own person and possessions."[4] Yet Locke does not make a point of the contradiction between these two descriptions. It is rather as if he had forgotten what he said earlier or perhaps lost his train of thought. Yet Locke does not seem to be a woolly-minded fellow, and his reputation shows that both his friends and his enemies take him seriously. His political thought typically contains contradictions, of which this one is perhaps the most important, but he leaves the reader to do the work of establishing the contradictions and working out their implications. In this case and in other cases, Locke does not leave the contradiction as flat as I have reported it; he teases readers with possible routes by which it might be harmonized.[5] But most

1. John Locke, *Two Treatises of Government* II 6, 27; see also I 30, 52–54, 85, 86; II 56.

2. Aristotle, *Politics*, 1254a10–12: A slave is one who belongs wholly to his master.

3. Locke, *Two Treatises* II 6.

4. Locke, *Two Treatises* II 123.

5. Locke deprecates the power of fathers over the children they beget; a father gets no right over his child by "the bare act of begetting." ("That's a joke, son," as Senator Claghorn of Allen's Alley used to say.) Children are not the property of fathers. One wonders, therefore, what the power of the Creator is over his creatures. Man being made in the image of his maker, he cannot but suppose he follows the will of his maker when he seeks his own self-preservation. Man has a self to preserve, and preserving it is in accordance with God's will. Well, then: God cannot have property in the image He made of Himself any more than a parent can have property in a child. Even if man is the workmanship

of all, Locke lets readers do their own harmonizing by allowing them to combine two things they want to believe. Almost all of Locke's readers would want to believe in the truth of Scripture, and many of them would like to think, or might be persuaded to think, that their belief is compatible with, or even entails, the notion of liberty that Locke sets forth.

The difference between belonging to God and belonging to yourself is not a small one. The opening question of the Heidelberg Catechism, a Reformation statement of Calvinist doctrine, says: "Q. What is your only comfort, in life and in death? A. That I belong—body and soul, in life and in death—not to myself but to my faithful Savior." Locke is sometimes said to be a Calvinist, and here is evidence of it; but the trouble is that he also shows evidence of the contrary. When he says that "every man has a property in his own person," he is starting the chapter on private property and opening his argument on the labor theory of value. Private property, it turns out, means property that belongs to human beings and not to God. When Locke speaks of charity from the rich to the poor, he makes it not a duty commanded by God but a right of the starving poor to the "surplusage" of the rich.[6] Here again Locke leaves a point to be noticed by those who can and want to notice, but he does not insist on it. How wise of him not to do so! The peace and prosperity of America depend on the peculiarly successful equivocation that Locke initiated between man's looking up to God and man's striking out on his own. What suffers somewhat is America's reputation for philosophical study and

---

of God, he cannot be the property of God; in fact, he follows the will of God when he regards himself as his own property. This is harmonization, not in the interest of religion, that submits the Bible to an argument for human liberty. See Locke, *Two Treatises* II 65 and the references in note 1.

6. Locke, *Two Treatises* I 42. See Thomas L. Pangle, *The Spirit of Modern Republicanism; the Moral Vision of the American Founders and of Locke* (Chicago, Ill.: University of Chicago Press, 1988), 144.

awareness of its principles.[7] "But a nation of philosophers is as little to be expected as the philosophical race of kings wished for by Plato."[8] This truth from the pen of Publius is a kind of guarantee that the harmonization between religion and liberty drawn from Locke by Americans was not the reasoning that Locke had in mind for himself.

Let us summarize the problem and its solution as Locke saw them. The workmanship argument makes man the work of God and thus establishes divine right over man, who though made in God's image remains the property of God, hence a slave. The self-ownership argument, by contrast, asserts that man is his own property, thus free and not a slave. The workmanship argument needs a notion of the soul as the conduit from God to man and the window through which man can see God (indistinctly, of course). But Locke hardly speaks of the soul in his work on political principles, *Two Treatises of Government*.[9] For Locke, it seems, the soul is the instrument of man's enslavement to an entity above himself insufficiently concerned with man's necessities, the necessities that require him to leave the state of nature and enter civil society. If man has a soul, then in Locke's view it would follow that he is neither free nor virtuous (for a slave has no virtue since virtue requires freedom). Instead of a soul, Locke supposes that man may have a "self," for the strongest desire in man is the desire for self-

7. "The Americans have no philosophic school of their own, and they worry very little about all those that divide Europe; they hardly know their names." Alexis de Tocqueville, *Democracy in America*, Harvey C. Mansfield and Delba Winthrop, trans. (Chicago, Ill.: University of Chicago Press, 2000), II 1.3, 403. In extenuation of Americans, however, it should be said that most Locke scholars today, for all their study and awareness of Locke, and despite their own lack of Christian faith, believe credulously in the credulity of Locke as if he in his harmonizing of faith and reason were no more perceptive than the average American.

8. *The Federalist* 49.

9. The two uses of the word in *Two Treatises* refer to the soul of the legislature (II 212) and to "mean souls" of slaves (II 239).

preservation.[10] And in the desire for preservation, the self is concerned with the body and seems limited by the wayward attractions
of the bodily senses. The senses are passive and receptive rather
than active, and they seem to lack any direction or integrity of
their own. Every time we think we are attending to something we
are actually merely being distracted by it, bombarded by impres-
sions of sense. Just as the soul is questionable because it yearns for
something divine, invisible to us, so the self is dubious because it
seems to be not a whole but a bundle of distractions. But Locke in
effect declares the self to have the substance that previously was
claimed for the soul, and in this way he combines divine right and
nondivine right. He seems to say: You can have self-preservation
without risking the salvation of your soul—or even instead of it.
Whichever. It's up to you.

Locke left a twofold legacy to America in regard to virtue and
liberty, offering compatibility and substitution. Virtue and liberty
could be compatible even if virtue is understood as obedience to
religion because man can be seen both as the workmanship of God
and as owner of himself. This appealed to the many devout and to
their preachers who wanted to both believe in God and live in
liberty. But also, as the self began quietly to substitute for the soul,
religion came to be subordinated to liberty. At the time of the
American Revolution several American colonies, turned states,
abolished the established church in their domains. Following
Locke, they could understand this measure as either a requirement
of or an undermining of true Christianity.

I will leave to others the description of Christian virtue as it
evolved to fit the requirements and enticements of Lockean liberty.[11] It must be stressed that the American virtue I am going to

10. Locke, *Two Treatises* I 86, 88; II 56.
11. See especially Barry Shain, *The Myth of American Individualism: The
Protestant Origins of American Political Thought* (Princeton, N.J.: Princeton University Press, 1994).

discuss was not the only, the average, or the majority virtue at the time of the founding. It was, however, the most typically American virtue because it was created by Americans at the time of the founding. Later on, this virtue was called by Tocqueville "self-interest well understood" and attributed to Americans as theirs.[12] In its private aspect, we find it in Benjamin Franklin's *Autobiography*; the public virtue can be seen in *The Federalist*.

Benjamin Franklin's Bourgeois Virtue

Bourgeois is not a word that Benjamin Franklin uses to describe virtue. If he had, it would have been one of the few times that the word has been used as a term of praise.[13] Bourgeois virtue was subjected to withering criticism from left and right throughout the nineteenth century, and the origin of it was a footnote in Jean-Jacques Rousseau's *Social Contract*, published in 1762, just nine years before Franklin started writing his autobiography. In the footnote, Rousseau distinguished a bourgeois from a citizen—a bourgeois being a town-dweller in the Middle Ages who received his freedom from a royal charter and a citizen being one who gave himself his own laws and who therefore had true, republican virtue.[14] Whereas republican virtue is honest, straightforward and naïve (and thus requires much strict education), bourgeois virtue is based on self-interest. According to Rousseau, self-interest sees itself as single-minded, sober, and sure, but in fact it is not. Self-interest is not one thing. If you think about it, you see that it is divided between what you yourself really want and what others want for you—and the latter tends to dominate. Thus, says Rous-

12. Tocqueville, *Democracy in America* II 2.8, 502.
13. I once remarked to my late colleague Judith Shklar that Americans' virtue is merely bourgeois virtue—to which she responded: "Is there any other kind?" I do not know whether she meant to praise the bourgeois or to denigrate virtue.
14. Jean-Jacques Rousseau, *On the Social Contract* I 6.

seau, you live for the sake of reputation with others rather than for self-satisfaction. A society devoted to self-interest actually turns into its opposite. You end up living in a society characterized by hypocritical politeness and pretense as opposed to liberty and virtue.[15] And although Franklin did not refer to Rousseau, his *Autobiography* constitutes a kind of answer to him. For Franklin thinks it is possible to be both self-interested and public-spirited.

Franklin's *Autobiography* is not merely an account of Franklin's life (as such, it would be quite inadequate). It is a book designed to teach moral lessons. It is written with reports and stories, mixing narration and dialogue like Franklin's favorite, John Bunyan's *Pilgrim's Progress*; and like that work, it is full of moral lessons, though much more worldly ones. Following John Locke, who besides his political and philosophical works wrote *Some Thoughts Concerning Education*, Franklin believed in liberty but did not leave to chance how liberty would be exercised. He saw that a liberal society needed virtue, and that for virtue, the society's citizens needed an education. One could not simply set men free and let them choose uninstructed. And whereas Locke argued for a private education by tutor for gentlemen, Franklin wanted a public education in public schools.[16] A private citizen, he takes it upon himself—in a

15. Two subsequent haters of the bourgeoisie, Max Weber and D. H. Lawrence, were virulent critics of Franklin's *Autobiography*. See Max Weber, *The Protestant Ethic and the Spirit of Capitalism*, Stephen Kalberg, ed. (Los Angeles, Calif.: Roxbury Press, 2002; German text originally published in 1904–5), 14–20; and D. H. Lawrence, *Studies in Classic American Literature* (New York: Thomas Seltzer, 1923). For fine recent studies of the *Autobiography*, see Ralph Lerner, *The Thinking Revolutionary: Principle and Practice in the New Republic* (Ithaca, N.Y.: Cornell University Press, 1987), 41–59, and *Revolutions Revisited: Two Faces of the Politics of Enlightenment* (Chapel Hill, N.C.: University of North Carolina Press, 1994), 3–18; Steven Forde, "Benjamin Franklin's Autobiography and the Education of America," *American Political Science Review* 86 (1992): 357–68.

16. For Franklin's educational writings, see Lorraine Smith Pangle and Thomas Pangle, *The Learning of Liberty: The Educational Ideas of the American Founders* (Lawrence, Kans.: University Press of Kansas, 1993).

free act of public spiritedness—to set himself up as an example, his book being addressed at first to his son. But then, we see later when Franklin includes two letters from friends praising what he had written in extravagant terms that it is intended for everyone ("think of bettering the whole race of men," says one friend).[17] A touch of vanity in Franklin, perhaps, to present himself as an example for mankind? But Franklin had anticipated this objection and had said at the beginning that he gives vanity "fair quarter wherever I meet with it," as it is "often productive of good" to the possessors and to those around him in his sphere of action.[18]

With this apology that is not an apology but a lesson, Franklin goes back over his life just as a printer goes back over a book looking, as it were, for typographical errors. It is customary to speak of the sins of one's past life, but Franklin calls them errata, finds five of them, and corrects them. He performs the office of St. Peter (or of God), judging his life and finding errors that were not so bad that they cannot be—not forgiven, but corrected. There is no display of vanity by Franklin, but also no show of humility. What sort of virtue does Franklin teach, then? He features sociability and public-spirited projects. He does not teach religion, though he does not oppose the teaching of religion. As a youth he wrote and printed a dissertation against religion, but luckily—or Providentially—he did not suffer for it. He began to "suspect that this [necessitarian] doctrine tho' it might be true, was not very useful."[19]

Franklin had "some religious principles"; he "never doubted" (despite what he admitted about his youthful disbelief) the exis-

---

17. Benjamin Franklin, *The Autobiography and Other Writings*, Kenneth Silverman, ed. (New York: Penguin Books, 1986), 84.
18. Franklin, *Autobiography*, 4.
19. Franklin, *Autobiography*, 63.

tence of God, and other essentials.[20] But he also had an objection
to religion as such: that it is contentious and polemical. He noticed
that from the first he was infected by books of "polemical divinity"
in his father's library that gave him a "disputatious turn," a very
bad habit making people often "very disagreeable in company."[21]
In short, religion tends to be unsociable. It sets people at odds and
sends nations to war. By contrast, human virtue is this-worldly,
which means mundane; it is about how to live in this world with
a view not to the next world but to this world. Virtue is not harsh;
it is sociable and conversational. Franklin says he learned how to
converse by reading about Socrates, who, he observed, preferred
to ask questions of rather than contradict his interlocutors.[22] But
Franklin, going Socrates one better, sought rather for "information" than learning, and while hiding his own view and raising sly
objections to another's, he made philosophy compatible with, or
even tantamount to, sociability. This modesty that is not really
modesty is just the sort of politeness that Rousseau detested.

Franklin's subtle modesty is on view in a passage where (*Autobiography*, p. 14), soon after admitting that he would have been "a
very bad poet," he presumes to correct the lines of the greatest poet
of the age, Alexander Pope. Pope had written:

> Immodest words admit of no defense,
> For want of modesty is want of sense.

20. Franklin, *Autobiography*, 89; the five essentials specified are the existence
of God; God's Providence; that man's most acceptable service to God is doing
good to man; that souls are immortal; that crime will be punished and virtue
rewarded here or hereafter. Note public spirit sitting comfortably and incon-
spicuously in the center of the list.

21. Franklin, *Autobiography*, 15.

22. Franklin, *Autobiography*, 18–19. And Socrates never embarrassed or
exposed the ignorance of anyone while asking his questions? And was never put
on trial and sentenced to death? Franklin, unlike Socrates, was able to embarrass
foolish acquaintances without risking death; see the incident in which he used
the "Socratic method" with Keimer, 39–40.

Franklin suggests that they would read better as:

> Immodest Words admit but this Defense
> That Want of Modesty is Want of Sense.

With this change, modesty receives "some apology," he says. In agreement with Socrates, Franklin implies that virtue is knowledge, and in disagreement with Socrates, that knowledge is about how to be sociable and so virtue is sociability. Sociability is useful, like religion.

There are many more beauties in Franklin's *Autobiography* that ought to be left to the reader to discover. Its theme is utility and the constant way to utility is through the suppression of one's ego, for that is the way to satisfy one's ego. Utility means utility to oneself, but not only to oneself, also to the public and to mankind. In his exemplary book, Franklin recounts a marvelous variety of useful projects in which he took the lead or provided the inspiration. It is as if he wanted to illustrate what Tocqueville was going to say about the art or science of association in America.[23] He could not have done all these things successfully, however, if he had done them out of crude, unadorned utility in the rule-bound manner of later utilitarians. He said that when swimming, he was "always aiming at the graceful & easy, as well as the Useful."[24] He himself was a man of style, and he wanted to give style to utility, or combine style with utility, lest life be made dull and crass.

The best part of style is not to attract attention. Franklin learned the impropriety of "presenting one's self as the Proposer of any useful Project"; it is much better to keep out of sight. "The present little Sacrifice of your Vanity will afterwards be amply repaid" when people find out that the credit belongs to you.[25] Yet three pages after saying this, Franklin presents as his own "the bold

---

23. Tocqueville, *Democracy in America* I 2.4; II 2.5–8.
24. Franklin, *Autobiography* 53; see Lerner, *The Thinking Revolutionary*, 43.
25. Franklin, *Autobiography*, 87.

and arduous Project of arriving at moral perfection." He had intended to write a book on the art of virtue, but instead he inserts only a couple of pages on twelve or thirteen virtues and precepts. He is no pompous Mr. Perfect, for these virtues are designed to improve him as well as others. They are formed on a method that seeks to prevent the usual fault of such a list that in focusing on one virtue a person tends to forget the other virtues. Franklin has a little book in which to record his faults, methodical fellow that he is. His list consists of bourgeois virtues to be sure, but also of citizen virtues such as justice and sincerity—thus spanning the distinction between bourgeois and citizen on which Rousseau insisted.

If we compare Franklin's list with the eleven virtues that Aristotle discusses in his *Ethics*, we see that Franklin has omitted courage, ambition, generosity, magnificence, magnanimity (Aristotle's magnanimous man, possessed of all the virtues and aware of it, would not keep a little book in which to write down his faults), friendliness, and wit. These are the virtues of nobility (except for friendliness and wit, virtues of sociability for its own sake rather than for utility), virtues that are out of the ordinary. To Aristotle's list Franklin adds virtues that are instrumental, such as order and cleanliness, that are beneath Aristotle's moral virtues. Franklin replaces Aristotle's generosity with frugality, the bourgeois virtue par excellence. Why so? He was a generous man, and if he was frugal it was so as to be generous. He was more than generous; he was a great man. But he does not "present himself" as such. His seventh virtue is sincerity, defined as "Use no hurtful deceit." Hmm. Is harmless or well-intended deceit what we usually mean by "sincerity"?

The *Autobiography* is chock-full of deceits that Franklin found not hurtful but useful.[26] It stops at the year 1757, just when Franklin

---

26. Lerner, *The Thinking Revolutionary*, 50–53.

was about to become a great man, entering the period of his life on which a biography would say the most. For Franklin's purpose it stops just at the right moment, for he did not want to look back on his life as from above. Even the scientific experiments he records show the human side of science—the vanity of scientists.[27] Franklin's cure for the vanity of the great man is to be kind and humane by disguising one's greatness. His book records what is today called the American Dream, a peculiar dream that can be realized. You make it real when you rise from poverty and obscurity by doing good for your fellow citizens. Franklin records the method for realizing the dream, which is to relax strict morality, not so much as to get ahead by fair means or foul, as with Machiavelli, but to get the approbation of other citizens, finally the public, who in general do not find strict morality attractive. Thus can a great man manage to survive among so many who are not great, and also benefit the community with many useful insights and inventions. But are these many useful benefits great benefits? On the first page of *The Federalist* it is said that America is an experiment for mankind to see whether good government can be established by reflection and choice, meaning republican government, rather than by accident and force. Here America is a great country because it provides a great benefit to mankind. We need to see how greatness presents itself in republican government.

Montesquieu on Republican Virtue

It might seem that republican government is not hospitable to greatness. Greatness is rare and great men are few; but republican government puts power in the hands of many rather than few. Republican government is distinguished above all from monarchy, which is government by one man. Traditionally, it was thought

27. Franklin, *Autobiography*, 172–73.

that republics would have to be small because only in a small country could the people run the government directly by meeting in a single popular assembly. The Anti-Federalists, who opposed the Constitution, accepted this "small-republic argument" while modifying it to allow a representative assembly elected by the people. So long as the terms of representatives were short and the turnover high, government would be close to the people if not identical with the people. To support their modified version of traditional republicanism, the Anti-Federalists relied for intellectual authority on Montesquieu, who in his *Spirit of the Laws* described the Greek cities as the paradigm of republicanism. In order to live peacefully, these cities had to be united, and for unity they needed to have one homogeneous people without ethnic or national divisions and a strict education to prevent factions from arising. Republics depend on virtue to stay united and to defend themselves against enemies, in contrast to monarchies, which have their unity in the monarch and which do not require virtue from either their subjects or the monarch.

What is this republican virtue? Montesquieu defined it to be strict, stern, austere, and even ascetic. He compared the virtue of republican citizens to the love that monks have for their order. Just as monks subordinate their particular interests when living together, so do citizens for the general good of the republic.[28] Virtue in this view is self-sacrifice, the very contrary of self-interest. After praising the republican virtue of the ancients, Montesquieu begins a critique of it that the Anti-Federalists failed to notice. Self-sacrifice, Montesquieu shows, requires an education that hardens citizens against enemies, producing martial virtue that he goes so far as to call "ferocity," followed by a countereducation in music that softens these same bellicose citizens so that they can

28. Montesquieu, *Spirit of the Laws* IV 6; V 2; XIV 7.

live with one another.[29] Montesquieu's idea of republican virtue perfects it by contrast to the virtue spoken of in the classical sources, because Plato and Aristotle always left room for a virtue above anything that could be achieved in politics.

Montesquieu, making a similar point for a different end, shows through careful stages of his argument that republican virtue cannot sustain itself and in the end destroys itself by trying to renounce and repress human interests and passions.[30] His solution is not to show the way to the higher virtue of philosophy but rather to lead his readers, disillusioned with republican virtue, toward a politics of liberty. In this new politics, no longer sought in the imagination but "found" in modern Britain, laws are mild, passions are loosed, interests are pursued, and commerce brings peace. The Anti-Federalists, wishing to follow Montesquieu but not quite taking his meaning, combined virtue and liberty by adding them together. They wanted both martial virtue and individual rights, and they did not fully appreciate the extent to which liberty was meant to replace virtue. They can be excused because Montesquieu did not make it clear either, and perhaps deliberately. A certain nostalgia for "ancient virtue" provides a prudent check on the selfish exploitation of commercial interests, on the one hand; and on the other, toleration of selfish passion takes the hard edge off righteous virtue. No matter that the boundary between virtue and liberty is not precisely defined.

Publius on Ambition

In *The Federalist*, however, a new outlook on "the extended republic" as opposed to the small republic makes possible a new republican virtue, one that can accommodate greatness. Ambition is the

29. Montesquieu, *Spirit of the Laws* IV 8.
30. The stages are summarized in my book, *Taming the Prince* (New York: The Free Press, 1989), 225–28.

focus of this new republicanism, and ambition leads to a new conception of responsibility. In one of many famous phrases in *The Federalist*, its pseudonymous author Publius says: "Ambition must be made to counteract ambition."[31] The context is a defense of the new form of separation of powers in the American Constitution, but the words might be quoted outside the context to apply to the whole society over which the Constitution will preside. Thus abstracted, we have a new principle connecting virtue to liberty. Franklin's *Autobiography* was all about ambition, but he left it off his list of virtues because he wanted ambitious people to defer to the doubt and envy of society and feared appearing too demanding of his fellow citizens' approbation. Publius, one could say, returns to Aristotle's promotion of ambition. Aristotle had noticed that people are blamed sometimes for too much, sometimes for too little ambition, as if there were an inconspicuous mean defining the right amount of ambition, the right degree of love of honor; so he proposed that this hitherto nameless quality be counted a virtue.[32]

Publius differs from Aristotle, however, in connecting ambition to interest rather than calling it a virtue. Just after saying that ambition must be made to counteract ambition, he adds that "the interest of the man must be connected to the constitutional rights" of the office, as if ambition were in one's interest. But is it in your interest to seek and accept public office? Many ambitious people decide not to run, as we know today; and there are theorists of "rational choice" who aver that following your own ambition is less rational than forgoing the honor yourself and taking a free ride on someone else's ambition. It does seem that ambition requires an expenditure of energy that might distinguish it from self-interest in its ordinary, less demanding forms, such as your

31. *The Federalist* 51.
32. Aristotle, *Nicomachean Ethics*, 1125b 1–25.

self-interest in a higher wage. In connecting ambition to interest, Publius shares Franklin's deference to popular, republican distrust of that quality (which he does not name a virtue); but in referring to ambition by name, he goes beyond Franklin. He seems to want to teach Americans that outstanding men of ambition are not so far from ordinary men as traditional republican suspicion supposes. Here is an example of what Tocqueville called the American doctrine of "self-interest well understood." Tocqueville remarked that in promoting that doctrine, Americans "would rather do honor to their philosophy than to themselves."[33] But in naming ambition, Publius goes a certain distance toward honoring it because he implies that it deserves to be singled out and provided for.

Let us recall that Publius mentions ambition while making a defense of the separation of powers. Ambition is asserted to be in the interest of the ambitious man, and his interest is connected to the constitutional rights of the office. *The Federalist* is renowned for the realism of its analysis, and especially for the famous argument in *The Federalist* 10 regarding "clashing interests." But the remedy proposed there is the extended republic, as opposed to a small, homogeneous democracy that allows one majority interest to dominate and oppress the country. This means that the play of interests is determined by the form of government. The interest of a faction differs in the two contexts: In the small republic it seeks to dominate and lord it over others; in the large, to conciliate and combine. These are two very different behaviors. An outside observer might want to call both of them self-interested, but if you were actually living in these two republics, you would say in the first that not to dominate is against your interest, and in the second, that domination is against your interest. The universality of self-interest, it seems, is too weak to specify how you should live. You

33. Tocqueville, *Democracy in America* II 2.8, 502.

need to know in addition what the political regime makes your interest to be. As a work of political science *The Federalist* could have been a dull tract of public law, for in outline all it does is explain the various parts and clauses of a formal document. Yet in saying why the Constitution was written as it was, Publius shows how he expects its offices to work. The realistic analysis enlivens, but also emerges from, the formal structure of the new proposed government.

In *The Federalist* 10, Publius warns against not only interests but also passions—against the "propensity of mankind to fall into mutual animosities [over] the most frivolous and fanciful distinctions." This might make one suppose that interests are solid and substantial, whereas passions are the contrary. It was common in the eighteenth century, as Albert Hirschman has shown, for philosophers and publicists to rely on solid interests to soothe excited passions. Hirschman begins his analysis from this leading quotation of Montesquieu: "Happily men are in a situation such that, though their passions inspire in them the thought of being wicked, they nevertheless have an interest in not being so."[34] But Montesquieu, sly fellow that he was, noted that passions might also inspire virtue, particularly the martial virtue characteristic of republics. This was the republican "ferocity" we have seen. He therefore took care in his book *The Spirit of the Laws* to gradually replace martial republican virtue with modern commercial self-interest. This is what Peter Berkowitz has nicely called "the healthy liberal impulse to economize on virtue."[35]

The Federalist goes along with the impulse for a considerable

---

34. Montesquieu, *Spirit of the Laws* XXI 20; Albert O. Hirschman, *The Passions and the Interests* (Princeton, N.J.: Princeton University Press, 1977). For my comments, see Harvey C. Mansfield, "Self-Interest Rightly Understood," *Political Theory* 123 (1995): 48–66.

35. Peter Berkowitz, *Virtue and the Making of Modern Liberalism* (Princeton, N.J.: Princeton University Press, 1999), 33.

distance, as Publius expects the American republic to be devoted to commerce rather than defensive or offensive war. But virtue will not be made obsolete. When discussing the House of Representatives, Publius declares that the aim of every political constitution is first to get rulers who discern and have the "virtue to pursue" the common good, and second to make precautions for "keeping them virtuous."[36] The virtue in question can only be public spirit or ambition. You might think that a virtuous person does not have to be kept virtuous, that virtue means being virtuous without external compulsion; but although this may be true of a few rare souls, it is too much to ask of the good men that voters can ordinarily hope to find, and above all with respect to the virtue of ambition. Ambitious men, we have seen, need to be counteracted by other ambitious men, but still perhaps as much to bring out their virtue as to prevent them from doing wrong.

When we come to the executive branch, Publius expands on the meaning of ambition, for the new American republic is not to have for its executive a committee chosen by the states, as in the Articles of Confederation, but a single person elected directly by the people. The U.S. Constitution establishes the first republic with a strong executive, and this office calls for a certain kind of person that is described in some detail. Publius goes so far as to deny directly "the maxim of republican jealousy which considers power as safer in the hands of a number of men than of a single man"—at least in regard to the emergencies that executive power must deal with.[37] But this advantage of one-man rule does not arise from superior virtue in him. The executive is held to be on the same level as ambitious men in the other branches, and though he might have "the stern virtue [that] is the growth of few soils"—like George Washington—it should be assumed that his virtue will not

36. *The Federalist* 57.
37. *The Federalist* 70.

be so exalted that he does not have to be "kept virtuous."[38] Accordingly, Publius organizes his account of the executive around a quality that has become very American, that most Americans today would consider a virtue—energy. "Energy in the executive is a leading character in the definition of good government." Again we see that the office calls for a certain character in the office-holder. Energy is a morally neutral term that comes from physics, and in *The Federalist* it is paired with its counterpart, stability. Any government, says Publius, needs both energy and stability, and the Framers had to make a special effort to combine them with the republican form, which in its traditional understanding had rarely achieved either.[39] Energy is something like ambition, except that ambition is ambivalent (you can have too much or too little, implying a mean that is the right amount and therefore a virtue) whereas energy is neutral and may be used for virtue or vice. Yet Publius uses the word as if energy were a virtue or led to virtue. One could say that for him, energy is understated virtue. To be a good executive you need to call on your own capacity for energy, and those who find themselves to be energetic will be the best for the job. The U.S. Constitution as a whole works through "job-based" virtues required for its various acting—or, better to say, counteracting—roles. It is not that nothing gets done, for though the government sometimes comes to a halt, the Constitution is not designed, as is sometimes said, for inaction or gridlock. The executive power is always ready to act in an emergency. And the supposed inaction of American government is better described as the action of one branch against a backdrop of counteraction by the two other branches of government.

What are the characteristics of energy that make for a good president? Speaking of the office, Publius says that the executive

38. *The Federalist* 73.
39. *The Federalist* 37.

needs to have unity: It must be one person rather than a committee. The reasons are that one person can act in emergencies without dissension and one person is more visible, hence more accountable than a committee. One could object that a committee could be unanimous and that one person might be of several minds and indecisive. Very true, which shows that the office requires a person who is decisive in emergencies, not merely one person of no particular character. One could go further and say that "decisive" is not enough either because the executive also must decide well. At this point, energy stops being neutral and becomes a virtue.

The next characteristic of energy is duration. Duration refers in the first place to time in office, the president having a four-year term that in the original Constitution could be extended indefinitely. Like unity, however, duration also refers to the character of the officeholder, to his not being a pushover, to his having "personal firmness."[40] He will have this because, having a long term, he may as well have it. Publius pronounces a "general principle of human nature" that a man will be "interested in whatever he possesses in proportion to the firmness of the tenure by which he holds it." A firm tenure does not merely call for but makes a firm man. The Constitution does not say of the executive office: only firm men need apply. It works through interest, using interest to produce virtue. Or would one again object that personal firmness is not necessarily a virtue because a person of this character might be a stubborn fool? The answer is that the executive will be enabled by the duration (and hence the independence) of his office to oppose the legislature, which being closer to the people is more likely to reflect "every sudden passion" or "every transient impulse" that may take hold of the people. The executive's personal firmness will prevent him from feeling or showing a "servile pliancy to a prevailing current," thus raising firmness above stubbornness.

40. *The Federalist* 71.

Here, too, energy shades into stability. A firm executive will have a stable administration.

We recall Franklin's list of virtues for a free society, which might be summed up as sociability under an aura of modesty. One of the virtues was resolution, in the sense of resolving to perform what one ought, not resolution against others. There is nothing like personal firmness in the list, and if you wanted to be critical, you could say it had an odor of servile pliancy to the opinion of society. Franklin gives us the virtues enabling us to live in a free society; Publius gives us the virtues for governing it. Both sets of virtues are characterized by modest understatement in which sternness and imperturbability in bad and good fortune are omitted or not stressed. Nothing heroic is set forth, much less required. But Publius sees, as against previous republican theorists, that in a popular government the virtue of standing up to the people is the most needful. Perhaps—and contrary to Franklin—personal firmness against the pressure of public opinion is the most useful social virtue as well. And you might get from the phrase *servile pliancy*, the contrary of personal firmness, the idea that there is something noble about it as well. Thus, when personal firmness is counted a political virtue, it might through imitation and emulation become a social one, too.[41]

There is a further stage in the meaning of energy, going beyond personal firmness, which arises when Publius takes up the lack of a constitutional limit on the president's eligibility for reelection. Interpreting this deliberate omission, Publius extends his discussion of duration from being firm to having long-range plans and goals—in Publius's always elegant prose, undertaking "extensive and arduous enterprises." And here Publius writes the famous phrase behind whose mask Alexander Hamilton's pen is obvious:

41. That George Washington understood this well is the point of Richard Brookhiser's fine book, *Founding Father: Rediscovering George Washington* (New York: Free Press, 1996).

"[L]ove of fame [is] the ruling passion of the noblest minds."[42]
The noblest minds are distinct from "the generality of men," and
as such not only must they be included but they must not be
excluded—as if the noblest minds had a right to a place in republican government. Not to allow them a second or third term would
be excluding them! For such a man would foresee that he could
not finish anything great that he might begin. Publius does not
refer to great men here, and the only man called "great" in *The
Federalist* is the philosopher Montesquieu.[43] But the American
people, perhaps prompted by professors, have taken up the game
of listing the "great presidents," and their presidents are by no
means indifferent to how they will "go down in history," which is
our subdued way of referring to the love of fame. It quite remarkable that America, a country so proud of its democracy, should be
so open to greatness. Of course, it democratizes greatness, so that
professional athletes, for instance, become "sports heroes" and are
awarded a place in some hall of fame. But it is no wonder that
when democracy recognizes greatness it democratizes greatness.
What is impressive is a democracy that, contrary to what might be
gathered from Benjamin Franklin's *Autobiography*, is willing to
recognize greatness (even if they often mistake it). I believe that
The Federalist and the form of government it defends have something to do with this fact. When Americans want to honor greatness they surely qualify their attachment to strict democratic
equality, but they do not have to leave the ambit of their republicanism. Thus they do not have to fall victim to a Napoleon.

Necessary to say—and how I wish it were needless to say—
American political science today is almost completely at a loss as
to how to appreciate the subtle interplay of interest and virtue in
The Federalist. The reason is that it cannot explain ambition or

42. *The Federalist* 72.
43. Hamilton, *The Federalist* 9.

public spirit and only thinks of reducing them to interest, desire for power, or aggression. But it is one thing to economize on virtue and quite another to replace it with economics.

Responsibility and Constitutional Space

We have not yet finished with the innovations of Publius in liberal virtue. In addition to ambition, an old topic, even discussed in Aristotle's *Ethics*, we find responsibility, a term newly applied, perhaps coined, by Publius to describe the correct behavior of a representative toward the people.[44] The word has caught on to the extent that today "fulfill your responsibilities" is the way we say "be virtuous" or "do your duty." This is the most striking example of *The Federalist*'s influence on our moral behavior and vocabulary.

Reference to responsibility as a virtue occurs principally in the discussion of the Senate, written by Madison, and of the president, written by Hamilton; but Madison is apparently the author of the new use of the word. Before *The Federalist*, being responsible meant being responsive, in the sense of being responsible to, and Madison introduced the idea of being responsible for. The House of Representatives, elected every two years, is more responsive to the people than is the Senate, yet the Senate, with its six-year term, allows a senator to become responsible for actions that the people might not think of on their own or endorse immediately but would approve in a more distant election or after things settle down. This relatively long term makes it possible for the government to sustain the difference between people's immediate desires and their deliberate sense, a distance that might be called constitutional space. In

44. See the excellent discussion, to which I am indebted, in David F. Epstein, *The Political Theory of the Federalist* (Chicago, Ill.: University of Chicago Press, 1984), 179–85. See also Douglass Adair, *Fame and the Founding Fathers*, T. Colbourn, ed. (New York: Norton, 1974), and Harvey C. Mansfield, "Responsibility and Its Perversions," in Andrew Cecil, ed., *Individualism and Social Responsibility* (Dallas, Tex.: University of Texas at Dallas Press, 1994), 79–99.

general, America has a popular government with constitutional space between the people and the government giving the latter freedom to act on behalf, as distinguished from at the behest, of the people. A responsible person uses this freedom to act on his own—taking the initiative or taking charge—in order to act on behalf of the people. The individual actor and the people are linked, and though the actor becomes outstanding in comparison with the rest of the people, even becomes something of a hero, he does not look down on the multitude of mere "human beings," as did Achilles.

Responsibility, like energy, is a morally neutral word because you can be the cause of, or be responsible for, evil as well as good. In everyday usage, however, responsible is a term of praise (like energetic), and irresponsible, a term of blame. It is linked to interest because it is in your interest to be known as responsible, but it also differs from interest. The responsible person takes a risk in acting, when by not taking charge, he might have let George do it and still reap the benefits or avoid the blame himself. Responsibility is a virtue that steps in when your interest is at a loss to decide between gaining a benefit and enduring some danger or being content to let things happen. It is voluntary, and less automatic than interest; and it makes one stand out from the rest rather than follow the average or mediocre course recommended by self-interest.

Responsibility is the virtue that makes possible the lack of virtue, or self-interest. It is the grander sense of freedom, the freedom to found and save a free country, that makes possible the generic sense of freedom, which is living as you please. Yet it is a democratic virtue, not because everyone will be responsible but because anyone can be. It is like a duty in being attached to an office or a role—the responsibility of the president or of a parent—but it differs from duty in being voluntary or, at least, more voluntary. Sometimes, as with a parent, the risk in responsibility is reduced to burden or inconvenience. Responsibility is the voluntary assumption of a task, like changing diapers, that you might not choose for itself. Even in a free country someone must change diapers—not a senator, of course, but someone with a virtue that encompasses the great and the menial.

To conclude: I have not been discussing the virtue of the majority of Americans at the time of the founding, for that would be more Christian and Protestant than what can found in the writings of Locke, Montesquieu, Ben Franklin, and the authors of *The Federalist*. My intent is to bring to light what was more innovative and at the same time more peculiarly American than what most Americans practiced and believed. Part of the innovation is in Franklin's list of virtues for a free, democratic society, in which religion is assumed but depreciated. More of the innovation, I would say, is in Publius, who is an underrated source of—one cannot say moral inspiration—moral suggestion and definition in America. Publius's notions of ambition, energy, and responsibility had behind them the force of the Constitution, the force deriving from the form, which provides constitutional space. What is this force? It is not self-interest generally or theoretically understood, but "the interest of the office." And the interest of the office is a kind of interest that permits and requires the cooperation of virtue. The lesson overall is that moral philosophy is incomplete without political philosophy.

T W O

Culture and
Values in
the 1960s

STANLEY KURTZ

The cultural revolution of the 1960s was both a fulfillment and a repudiation of the vision of America's founders. The Civil Rights Movement of the early 1960s extending the rights of full citizenship to individuals regardless of race, sex, or creed was a culminating and long overdue realization of the principle of human freedom and equality enshrined in the Declaration of Independence. That struggle, in turn, served as a prototype for movements of women's liberation, gay rights, protection of the natural environment, and activities in sympathy with liberation movements in the Third World. Yet the legacies of these latter movements (and even of the post-1960s civil rights movement) are matters of active dispute in contemporary America.

Virtually all Americans now agree that the end of legal segregation, the achievement of legal equality for women, increased social tolerance for homosexuality, concern for the environment, and heightened respect for non-Western cultures are welcome achievements of the 1960s. Each of these achievements can legitimately be seen as an expression of the spirit of individual freedom and human equality at the heart of the founders' liberalism.

Yet it also is arguable (and many have made the argument) that important strands within each of these movements, however apparently liberal in form and intent, have gone well beyond the charter of liberalism as understood by America's founders. Even granting this, a mystery remains. If the movements that began in the 1960s have in some significant measure departed from classic liberalism, how are we to understand their inner rationale? What connects the ecology movement, for example, with movements for civil rights? And if classic liberalism no longer suffices for many Americans, what has prompted them to set it aside?

It is difficult, if not impossible, to offer an answer to these questions without becoming an active disputant in this nation's ongoing and unresolved clash over the cultural legacy of the 1960s. Any characterization or explanation of the sixties revolution tends either to credit or to undermine the self-understanding of the cultural revolutionaries themselves. Certainly the explanation and characterization of the sixties ethos that I offer here implies considerable skepticism about the self-understanding of the bearers of the sixties legacy. I argue that the sixties ethos, and the transformation of liberalism it has produced, is best understood as a secular religion, and in many respects an illiberal religion. That the legacy of the 1960s may be in important respects illiberal is a profoundly troubling fact for those who value the heritage of America's founders and the achievements of the struggle for civil rights in the 1960s.

If there is an element of polemic in this attempt to make sense of the 1960s, therefore, I maintain that it is unavoidable. Perfect neutrality in the human sciences is neither possible nor desirable. When the topic is the fundamental fissure in the culture of the present, that truth is still more applicable, or at least more evident. Nonetheless, it is important (and liberal) to note that the insights offered here are available to the scrutiny and criticism of those they criticize. In fact, it is in no way difficult to imagine partisans of the sixties ethos enthusiastically embracing my point that the legacy of that era now functions as much as a religion as a political theory. Indeed, as will become evident, insight into the religious significance of a transformed liberalism originates with one of liberalism's great nineteenth-century proponents. Even my point that the sixties ethos disguises a deep illiberalism will be unsurprising, and in some respects unobjectionable, to postmodernists who have consciously criticized and rejected classic liberal thought.

From a perspective different from postmodernism, I shall argue that the liberalism of many children of the 1960s betrayed itself by becoming an illiberal religion. After describing the core symbolic dynamic of this very modern religion, I shall trace the political and intellectual roots of the quasi-religious ethos of the 1960s and offer some thoughts about the sources of this important cultural shift.

Liberalism As Religion

Sometime during the past thirty years, liberalism stopped being a mere political perspective for many people and turned into a religion. I do not speak metaphorically. A certain form of liberalism now functions for substantial numbers of its adherents as a religion: an encompassing world-view that answers the big questions about life, dignifies daily exertions with higher significance, and provides a rationale for meaningful collective action.

It wasn't supposed to be that way. Liberalism arose as a solution to the destructive religious wars of Europe's past and succeeded because it allowed people of differing religious perspectives to live peacefully and productively in the same society. Designed to make the world safe for adherents of differing faiths, liberalism itself was never supposed to *be* a faith. But to a significant extent, that is what liberalism has become. In this new, transformed mode, it is perhaps more accurate to refer to left-liberalism than to liberalism per se, for classical liberalism—the liberalism of Locke, Montesquieu, Madison, and Mill—remains an accessible and viable alternative. Nevertheless, the transformation of liberalism into a de facto religion for many explains the dynamics of something we have come to call political correctness, that controversial cultural inheritance of the late 1960s.

The central mechanism of political correctness is the stigmatization of perspectives, many of them classically liberal, that run afoul of left-liberalism—a condemnation disproportionate to what might be expected in matters of mere policy disagreement. However balanced, well-reasoned, or rooted in long-established principle objections may be to, say, affirmative action, traditional (indeed, classically liberal) viewpoints on these and other issues are often stigmatized as racist, sexist, and homophobic—that is, as bigotry unfit for reasoned debate. This shift to ostracism in place of intellectual engagement in so many of our cultural debates cannot be explained as a mere conscious tactical maneuver. The stigmatization of traditional perspectives can only be effective because so many are primed to respond to it in the first place.

Why, then, have so many classic objections to left-liberal perspectives been demonized? Possibly because liberalism has become a religion in need of demons. Traditional liberalism emphasized the ground rules for reasoned debate and the peaceful adjudication of political differences. One of the main reasons that politics in a liberal society could be peaceful was that people sought direction about life's ultimate purpose outside of politics itself. But once traditional religion ceased to provide many moderns with either an ultimate life-purpose or a pattern of virtue, liberalism itself was the only belief system remaining that could supply these essential elements of life.

How, then, does liberalism (transformed into post-1960s left-liberalism) grant meaning to life? How does it do what religion used to do? So long as it serves as a mere set of ground rules for adjudicating day-to-day political differences, liberalism remains too "boring" to serve as a religion. But what if liberals were engaged at every moment in a dire, almost revolutionary, struggle for the very principles of liberalism itself? What if liberals were at war on a daily basis with King George III? with Hitler? with Bull Connor? *That* would supply a purpose to life—a purpose capable of endowing even our daily exertions with a larger significance, and certainly a purpose that would provide a rationale for meaningful collective action.

Consider two important features of contemporary left-liberalism: the continual expansion in meaning of terms like *racism*, *sexism*, and *homophobia* and the tendency to invent or exaggerate instances of oppression. Whereas *racism* once meant the hatred of someone of another race, the term is now freely applied to anyone who opposes affirmative action, or even to anyone who opposes reparations for slavery. Again, this stigmatization of what were once mainstream liberal positions makes a certain amount of tactical sense, but the tactics don't really explain the phenomenon.

The young students who now live in ethnic/cultural theme houses or who join (or ally themselves with) ethnic/cultural campus political organizations are looking for a home, in the deepest sense of that word. In an earlier time, the always difficult and isolating transition from home to college was eased by membership in a fraternity or by religious fellowship. Nowadays, ethnic/cultural theme houses, political action, and related course work supply what religion and fraternities once did.

Yet if the ethnic/cultural venture is truly to take the place of religion, it must invite a student to insert himself into a battle of profound significance. The fight for slave reparations and the unceasing effort to ferret out examples of subtle racism in contemporary society are techniques for sustaining a crusading spirit by creating the feeling that Simon Legree is lurking just around the corner. Opponents of affirmative action or slave reparations simply must be imagined as monsters. Otherwise the religious flavor of the multiculturalist enterprise falls flat, and the war of good against evil is converted into difficult balancing of competing political principles and goods in which no one is a saint or a devil.

Consider the tendency of contemporary cultural movements to invent oppression—as, for example, in ongoing (yet long since debunked) feminist statistical claims about campus rape, economic discrimination, and the alleged educational crisis of adolescent girls.[1] These questionable statistics are not incidental, but are critical to the feminist cause. So many of the young women who affiliate themselves with campus women's centers are looking for a world-view, a moral-social home, and a meaningful crusade in which to take part. That is why the horrifying (if often false) statistics of female oppression purveyed by these centers conjure up—and are meant to conjure up—images of slavery and the Holocaust.

Betty Friedan's *The Feminine Mystique* was a powerful book because it characterized the suburban home as a "comfortable concentration camp" for women.[2] Friedan's repeated use of Holocaust metaphors for the alleged oppression of women is of a piece with the contemporary feminist practice of making exaggerated or false statistical claims. The Holocaust imagery and the frightening statistics are meant to endow the feminist crusade with an almost apocalyptic sense of urgency and significance. Statistical accuracy

1. For critiques of these claims, see Diana Furchtgott-Roth and Christine Stolba, *The Feminist Dilemma* (Washington: The AEI Press, 2001); Christina Hoff Sommers, *Who Stole Feminism?* (New York: Simon & Schuster, 1994); Christina Hoff Sommers, *The War Against Boys* (New York: Simon & Schuster, 2000).

2. See Betty Friedan, "Progressive Dehumanization: The Comfortable Concentration Camp," chap. 12 in *The Feminine Mystique* (New York: Dell, 1963).

is less important here than creation of a cause, a fellowship, a reason for being.

Of course, to say that liberalism in the hands of left-liberals has ceased to be a political perspective and has become an intolerant religion is another way of saying that liberalism has betrayed itself and become illiberal. This point is nicely made by Brian C. Anderson in "Illiberal Liberalism."[3] Anderson shows how the persistent attempts to silence and stigmatize conservative views by even mainstream liberal voices betray the commitment to rational and civil debate at the core of genuine liberalism. To the extent that liberalism itself functions as an illiberal religion, the principles that made liberalism what it was—principles like free speech, reasoned debate, and judicial restraint in the face of democratic decision making—are left by the wayside.[4] The secular religion of a significant share of today's educated elite is still recognizable as an outgrowth of classic liberalism. Yet underneath talk of "rights" and "oppression," we are often faced with a very modern way of reproducing the classic religious dichotomies of good versus evil, and us against them.

Many distinguished thinkers have chronicled the story of America's growing and dangerous tendency toward individual isolation.[5] That story is largely true, yet it is also incomplete. We cannot

3. Brian C. Anderson, "Illiberal Liberalism," *City Journal* 11, no. 2 (spring 2001).

4. This should not be taken to imply that religion, as such, is "bad." Liberalism and religion are, or should be, different things. Liberalism's attention to fair procedure for those of differing world-views is, by nature, something that depends upon toleration. Moreover, as will become evident below, the religious characteristics of the sixties ethos tend to congeal paradoxically into an orthodoxy while eschewing the ethic of sacrifice that is a characteristic strong point of traditional religion. So the problems with left-liberalism as a political religion in no way imply that religion, in and of itself, is bad or for that matter illiberal.

5. See Alexis de Tocqueville, *Democracy in America* (New York: Harper Perennial, 1969); Allan Bloom, *The Closing of the American Mind* (New York: Simon & Schuster, 1987); Francis Fukuyama, *The End of History and the Last Man* (New York: Avon, 1992); *Habits of the Heart: Individualism and Commit-*

bear our isolation. So in ways sometimes hidden even from our-selves, we strive to overcome it. Left-liberalism as religion is one solution to the problem of life in a lonely secular world. It allows one to appear to be fighting for individual freedom without quite acknowledging to oneself that one has enlisted in a grand, collec-tive, and frequently intolerant religious crusade.

But if classic liberalism transformed into left-liberalism now functions as an intolerant religion, in what sacred iconography is the new creed embodied? Betty Friedan's foundational feminist work, with its attack on the 1950s suburban home as a "comfort-able concentration camp," suggests an answer.

The Holocaust Metaphor

The Holocaust has become our moral touchstone—the most important cultural symbol of our era. That is a problem. The Jewish Holocaust of World War II was a human tragedy on a scale that beggars description. Serious study of the Holocaust and meditation upon this terrible event by the general public are most necessary and worthy endeavors. Yet can the Holocaust be made to serve as the chief organizing principle of our moral universe? For many of those influenced by the spirit of left-liberalism, it already does.

In a relativist age, the Holocaust serves for many as a moral anchor. Forty years ago, preoccupation with the Holocaust was still considered morbid, and the moral lesson it taught remained something of a debaters' point. We knew, when pressed, that if nothing else was immoral the Holocaust was. Yet we did not yet know how to turn the Holocaust into an engine of meaning. Many learned. Perhaps because they had to. Human beings crave moral certainty. If the Holocaust had waved us away from moral certainty

---

ment in *American Life*, ed. Robert Bellah et al. (Berkeley: University of California Press, 1996), updated edition; Robert Putnam, *Bowling Alone: The Collapse and Revival of American Community* (New York: Simon and Schuster, 2000).

for fear of committing horrors in the name of some higher cause, then for many, the Holocaust would itself, of necessity, become the key to moral certainty. But how? How could a debaters' point become a way of life? It became necessary to learn how to use the Holocaust to actually generate meaning. And having mastered this, many would learn how to recognize "little Holocausts" everywhere. All too frequently, the world would accommodate this need for little Holocausts. When it did not, they could use their imaginations.

Weighed down by a sense of the banality of their existence, the baby boomers were given a life of material comfort but longed instead for a life of exertion in the service of some larger purpose, or at least for the appearance of such a life. The solution hit upon by many was to identify with struggling groups—however temporarily, however superficially, however counterproductively. Student involvement in the early movement for civil rights was the entirely praiseworthy prototype of this moral pattern, but the many later attempts to copy that original crusade were troubling in character.

The post-1960s proliferation of civil rights crusades had the effect of frequently dividing the world into tyrants and victims, and a shallow but ostentatious appropriation of the victim's superior prestige created what was, in effect, a new aristocracy of suffering. Heightened sensitivity to prejudice, or apparent prejudice, would become the keynote of the new identities because, over and above a few affected markers, no belief or way of life actually distinguished American blacks, women, or Jews—or any given ethnic group—from anyone else.

The new ethnicity seemed to operate as a way of associating individuals with some larger community. More deeply, however, the new ethnicity was a form of self-cultivation. Pasting together a series of identities, preferably rebellious and often fleeting, was more a way of distinguishing oneself from the mass than of forging

stable connections to a given community. And yet, more paradoxically still, the gesture of suffering rebellion had itself become
obligatory—a required ritual of admission to a society in which
everyone became an individual in precisely the same way.[6]

The denial of freedom—or better, life—to an innocent multitude serves as the sacred icon of our time. The new goal is to
identify oneself with mass-scale suffering and to strive to prevent
it. On the face of it, of course, any such horror rightly calls forth
our outrage. The fact that we are stirred to action by collective
oppression or mass killing seems transparently to be our obligation, not some novel religion. Christ on the cross, after all, long
the West's most potent icon, is the very image of blameless suffering. Yet the crucifixion is more than a picture of innocent agony.
It is a paradigm of sacrifice—of a God who so loved the world that
he gave to it, and willingly lost to it, his only begotten son. The
displacement of the icon of Christ by the Holocaust metaphor
marks a cultural shift of considerable significance.

Many are now unable to work within the old paradigm of
sacrifice, or even to recognize or comprehend it. This is reflected,
for example, in the diminishing ability of young Catholics to find
vocations as nuns or priests and in the incomprehension of those
who are disinclined to, say, accept marital advice from a celibate
priest. For many, the connection between Jesus' sacrifice of his life,
the sacrifice entailed in celibacy, and the sacrifice at the heart of
marriage has been lost.

We've already seen how feminism constitutes a kind of modern
religion built around Holocaust metaphors, broadly construed
(not simply Friedan's "comfortable concentration camp" theme,
but also, for example, the—unsubstantiated—idea of a vast epi-
demic of rape). But the purest example of the Holocaust meta-

6. This portion of my account of the sixties ethos draws on Alain Finkiel-
kraut, *The Imaginary Jew* (Lincoln: University of Nebraska Press, 1994 [1980]).

phor's operation in contemporary leftist thinking is found in the eco-terrorism movement.

Concern for the environment, of course, is one of the great positive legacies of the 1960s. Nonetheless, in the extreme form of eco-terrorism, a welcome concern for the environment is transformed into something more problematic. Precisely because of its extremism, eco-terrorism allows us to see, with particular clarity, the operation of the Holocaust metaphor within the religion of left-liberalism.

Eco-terrorism, sponsored by loosely knit groups like the Animal Liberation Front and Earth Liberation Front, began in earnest in 1998, with the burning down of a mountaintop ski resort in Vail, Colorado, the release of 10,000 minks from an Oregon mink farm, and the burning of a slaughterhouse. Eco-terrorism has proliferated since then, although, until recently, fear of provoking further retaliation has prevented targeted businesses from publicizing the problem. Biotechnology projects are the latest targets, with a fire set to the offices of a global biotech project at Michigan State University in Lansing in 1999 and various experimental crop sites elsewhere destroyed.[7]

The attacks are sometimes mistaken (for example, targeting scientists who are not in fact engaged in bioengineering) and often counterproductive, the attacks themselves backfiring politically on the activists (for example, released minks die in the wilderness). But as is characteristic of left-liberalism as religion, it is the feeling of being a rescuer that counts, not the reality.

The iconography of these activists is Holocaust iconography—photos of animals being experimented on or locked away in small cages. The release of the minks and the burning of the slaughterhouse resemble nothing so much as our dream of preventing the

7. "Eco-vandals put a match to 'progress,'" *Christian Science Monitor* (July 5, 2001).

Holocaust. In fact, the Animal Liberation Front explicitly invokes the image of U.S. soldiers liberating Jews from Nazi death camps to justify its actions.

Of course, a great deal depends upon whether we accept the analogy between animals and humans. Yet the question of the moral status of animals actually serves to disguise the underlying religious and illiberal significance of eco-terrorism. The eco-terrorists have a very particular way of equating animals and humans, different from most of us. For example, although vegetarian, many Hindus see animals in an entirely different way than do the eco-terrorists. Hindus worship the cow as the embodiment of motherly sacrifice and the monkey as a symbol of manly self-control and power.

Things are different in the new political religion. Here animals embody no socially authorized pattern of sacrifice. They are, on the contrary, mute victims, whose relative incapacity only serves to ratify the purity of their victimhood. The credibility of any human claim of oppression can always be called into question, but a mass of mute animals is the perfect image of large-scale innocent suffering—a perfect little Holocaust just waiting to be prevented.

What of animals' disturbing tendency to consume one another? This muddying of the moral waters has been nicely circumvented, by the LLF (Lawn Liberation Front), which, in 2001, distributed fliers to homeowners in a Pittsburgh suburb claiming that 12-inch spikes may have been driven into their lawn to stop them from cutting the grass.[8] "Grass is a living entity that deserves as much respect as humans," said the fliers. So nostalgia for the heroism of World War II can now take the form of action to prevent the genocide of millions of blades of innocent grass. In an ultimate bid to spread the new religion, every man is now offered the

---

8. *Pittsburgh Post-Gazette*, "Group's Unkind Cut Targets Mowers," July 5, 2001.

opportunity to prevent a holocaust from taking place, quite literally, in his own backyard.

Few eco-terrorists get caught. The risks are minimal, but the sense of moral superiority substantial. And such sacrifice as is entailed in the risk of criminal prosecution is dramatically different from the sacrifice embodied in the old religious mode. Eco-terrorists operate in isolated cells of individuals around the country, few of whom know one another's identity. This is not the sort of sacrifice that builds families and communities. It is a simulacrum of sacrifice, undertaken to rescue the children of today's suburban affluence from the oppressive sense of being ordinary.

The physical destruction of university research is perhaps the clearest example we have of the implications of political correctness for academic freedom. But the threat of eco-terrorism goes deeper. Intelligence analysts worry that the history of violence combined with the ideology of *deep ecology*, which holds that human civilization has to be rolled back until the earth's natural environment is fully restored, may lead to the use of large-scale weapons of mass destruction (especially biological warfare) by eco-terrorists. Ironically, those who seek to prevent sham holocausts create a rationalization for perpetrating holocausts of their own.

The real significance of eco-terrorism, however, is the clarity with which it reveals the larger tendencies of the contemporary religion of left-liberalism. This religion works by seizing upon, exaggerating, distorting, and inventing images of mass-scale death and oppression. The point of this religion is not to gain salvation or power through self-discipline and sacrifice, but to achieve a feeling of moral superiority through attempts to stave off potential holocausts. The goal, in a sense, is to make every man a Schindler.

The majority of environmental activists eschew violence, and the public at large favors well-lit houses and SUVs. Yet the Holocaust metaphor is alive and well even in mainstream political battles over the environment, such as the dispute over drilling in

the Arctic National Wildlife Reserve (ANWR). The debate over
drilling plans is more than a complex effort to balance environmental sensitivity with the nation's evident need and desire for
energy. Inevitably, the proposal to drill in the ANWR invokes a
kind of collective shudder—a feeling that whatever the safeguards,
whatever the need for energy, drilling in the ANWR is like a little
Holocaust. The debate over the ANWR may seem to turn on issues
of public policy, but it's really a theological skirmish in the ongoing
war between two American cultures and their respective religions.

Durkheim and the Origin of the New Religion

How shall we understand the rise of this new and illiberal religion?
Our propensity to forge solidarities with the oppressed is an offspring of the world-view conceived by Marx. Yet the new religious
sensibility is better understood as an outgrowth of developments
first identified by Emile Durkheim, one of the founders of modern
sociology. Durkheim was raised in a strictly observant Orthodox
Jewish household, son of the district's chief rabbi and scion of a
long line of rabbis.[9] He was expected to follow in his father's
footsteps, but he lost his faith, then instead set out to gain admission to the Ecole Normale Supérieure, the premier institution of
higher learning in France. Living in Paris, studying to gain admission to the Ecole Normale, Durkheim twice failed his exams. He
endured three years of anguished isolation before finally securing
a place at the school.

Durkheim's work is a sociological autobiography of sorts. He
was preoccupied with the transition of traditional social forms,
governed by a comparatively stable consensus on the details of
ordinary living, into complex modern societies. For Durkheim,

9. For an excellent account of Durkheim's life and the direction of his
thought, see Steven Lukes, *Emile Durkheim: His Life and Work* (New York:
Penguin, 1977 [1973])

the increasing differentiation of social roles demanded by modern life had the inevitable effect of weakening moral consensus and highlighting the differences among individuals. What could hold society together under the pressure of such vocational and moral differentiation? Durkheim's initial answer was that the same pro-liferation of complex tasks that heightens individuality and under-mines consensus itself creates a form of interdependence.[10] A contemporary telecommuter, for example, may stay at home, through his computer and modem. Yet the very uniqueness of his task forces him to depend upon an array of computer specialists and, ultimately, upon the government that regulates the electronic infrastructure. The difficulty is that this sort of pragmatic inter-dependence is hardly a substitute for the sense of shared moral purpose typical of homes and communities suffused by traditional religious belief.

Durkheim understood this, and so was preoccupied with find-ing a way to recapture, in modern form, the communal spirit that had been lost with the passing of traditional religion. For Durk-heim himself, his time at the Ecole Normale Supérieure had achieved that purpose. In the late nineteenth century, the Ecole Normale Supérieure was a tightly regulated institution. Students would be locked inside for days on end, but they would spend this time together in a kind of hothouse of intellectual interchange and fellowship. Here there was both a common purpose and a pre-mium placed on individual innovation—a synthesis of the old and the new. For Durkheim, this was the solution, and in the years following his graduation, he built around himself a circle of col-laborators that tended to reproduce the atmosphere of the school. As his thinking developed, Durkheim experimented with propos-als for large-scale, occupationally based corporations—mid-range

---

10. The aspect of Durkheim's thought discussed here is set forth in Emile Durkheim, *The Division of Labor in Society* (New York: The Free Press, 1984).

associations between the individual and government, to be given
real legislative responsibility, and out of which some common
spirit might emerge to heal the rift between labor and management.
Yet little came of this attempt to split the difference between capitalism and socialism.

Throughout his career, Durkheim conceived Europe to be in
a state of transition toward a new moral consensus. He saw no
reason to believe that societies of the future would be incapable of
producing some new moral faith, resembling those of the past, yet
better suited to the needs of modern life. Despite his attempts to
imagine a resurgence of community centered around occupational
corporations, Durkheim continued to believe that the forging of a
new morality could not be "improvised in the silence of the study."
On the contrary, it had to grow of its own, out of the unfolding
development of society itself—although having thus emerged, it
could be recognized and shaped.

At one critical moment of his career, Durkheim came to feel
that he had, after all, caught a glimpse of what this religion of the
future might be. And much as Durkheim anticipated, this realization emerged, not from the silence of the study, but under the
pressure of outside events. At the turn of the century, the infamous
Dreyfus affair exposed a rift in French society quite as profound
as the conflicts that broke out in America in the 1960s. Alfred
Dreyfus, the sole Jewish officer in the upper reaches of the French
military, was falsely accused of treason and exiled to Devil's Island
on the basis of forged evidence. As the fabrications began to
unravel, the intellectuals of France joined forces with secular liberals and religious minorities in opposition to the conservative
monarchists and traditional Catholics who supported the verdict.
Emile Zola's famous "J'accuse" signaled the beginning of the intellectuals' assault on the conservatives, an offensive that Durkheim
himself soon joined—the only time in his career he took active
part in an ongoing political controversy.

As a secular Jew who now saw, not the community of his fathers, but France itself as his home, Durkheim identified with Dreyfus. If anti-Semitic suspicions could bar Jews from the army, none could advance within society at large. But what really drew Durkheim out of his study and into the fray was an argument made by the opponents of Dreyfus in answer to the increasingly shrill protests of Zola and his friends. So what if Dreyfus was innocent, went this argument of the conservatives. To admit this would be to embarrass and undermine the Church and the army— institutions that had supported Dreyfus's conviction and whose authority was essential for the proper functioning of society. The plight of a single individual could not be permitted to overbalance the interests of the country as a whole. From this conservative perspective, it was the individualism of the intellectuals, and not the regrettable fate of Dreyfus himself, that posed the true danger to France.[11]

Durkheim's public answer to this argument provoked a new train in his thought. His initial view had been that the transition to a role-differentiated, and therefore individualistic, society por- tended an inevitable weakening of moral consensus—the shift to a morally shallow pragmatic interdependence. That meant a weak- ening of religion as well because for Durkheim, religion was, in essence, the symbolic expression of an underlying moral consen- sus. But now Durkheim realized that even in modern society, moral consensus (and thus religion of a sort) never completely fades away. In effect, the primacy of the individual, itself the outcome of our shattered social unity, now becomes our religion—the cen- ter of our reconstructed moral life. In the absence of relative agree- ment on the details of everyday living, our belief in the sacred character of the individual constitutes the last remaining basis for

11. Emile Durkheim, "Individualism and the Intellectuals," in *Emile Durk- heim: On Morality and Society*, ed. Robert N. Bellah (Chicago: University of Chicago Press, 1973).

our collective moral (and thus religious) life. So Durkheim was able to turn the argument of the conservatives around. According to Durkheim, it was actually the anti-Dreyfus forces that threatened social anarchy. In Durkheim's eyes, the conservatives were undermining the new secular religion of modernity (the religion of individual rights) by sacrificing the rights of Dreyfus to the interests of the Church and the army.

A hundred years ago, this was not obvious. The rights of man, of course, had been the centerpiece of the French Revolution, but the Cult of the Supreme Being, a religion contrived by the revolutionaries as a celebration of those rights, had been something of a flop with the public. So instead of jettisoning traditional religion in favor of a formal religion of rights, the revolutionary tradition entered into a state of protracted struggle with the forces of social and religious tradition. For a very long time, few would have dared to call the belief in human equality and liberty our de facto religion. Indeed it is evident that Durkheim himself was far from believing that the idea of universal human rights could, without supplement, evolve into a moral tradition rich enough to alleviate the isolation and alienation characteristic of modernity. To the end of his life, Durkheim continued to anticipate the development of some novel form of moral community—a community that could heal the wounds inflicted by modernity while remaining compatible with modernity's complex vocational structure. Nonetheless, drawing on the tradition of the Revolution itself, Zola, Durkheim, and their compatriots had been present at the creation of the modern intellectual dissident, the social outsider who challenged tradition and authority in the name of liberty, equality, and the society of the future. This politically active intellectual was an early carrier of the new religion of liberalism.

Yet the larger social and moral constellation that Durkheim both expected and longed for never materialized. Or did it? Our modern Communitarians, descended, many of them, from Durkheim, continue his attempt to envision and nurture new or reformed communal moralities. In the meantime, something interesting has emerged among the postmodern *critics* of communitarianism. The tradition of the dissident intellectual, with his religion of human rights, has itself taken on far greater moral significance than even Durkheim imagined it would. In the process, this tradition of dissidence has been transformed. In effect, the tradition of the individual (and individualist) dissident has itself become the locus of our hidden communal strivings—with ambiguous results.

Durkheim was looking to re-create the close-knit Jewish community of his youth in a modern context. The tight discipline and common intellectual life of the Ecole Normale Supérieure had done this for him, relieving the alienation of his years of study alone in Paris. By 1968, the number of young people leaving their home communities to attend college had increased enormously— a surefire recipe for Durkheimian alienation (now called identity crisis). Yet, unlike Durkheim, the demonstrators of 1968 were hardly looking to recapture the pleasures of a youth spent in communal religious devotion. Their upbringing had been notably materialistic and free. At college they demanded more of the same. One of the sparks of the big Paris demonstrations, for example, was an attempt by school officials to punish a girl for rooming with her boyfriend. Similar incidents helped spark demonstrations in the United States. Students at the climactic Parisian demonstrations were told that there were to be no marshals—no one to govern the conduct or direction of the marchers. They were to be *their own* marshals—seemingly the antithesis of Durkheim's tightly regulated life at the Ecole Normale Supérieure.

Durkheim was convinced that, appearances to the contrary, no one is ever really his own marshal. To be utterly without socially imposed discipline, to be free of all normative regulation, to be under the authority of oneself alone, is to be plunged into *anomie*—

a crisis of aimless or infinite desire. The ultimate outcome of complete freedom and undirected individual desire is, Durkheim maintained, suicide. To ask incessantly, "What is the meaning of *my* life," can end only in death. Instead, Durkheim insisted, recognize it or not, we remain in life only insofar as we ask "What is the meaning of *our* life—here, now, in this society?"[12]

So the students who rejected Durkheim's belief in the need for some collective moral "discipline" would, of necessity, have had to restore it in some subterranean fashion. They did so in several ways. The hothouse of social and intellectual interchange that Durkheim found within the locked gates of the Ecole Normale Supérieure was re-created in heated meetings on strategy and ideology, now held within buildings taken over and barred from the inside by the students themselves. And the object of protest was no mere individual denied his rights. Rights were still the keynote, but now the rights to life and liberty of whole peoples were at stake, peoples whose collective identities could thus be vicariously, if temporarily, appropriated. This pattern had been implicit even in the Dreyfus affair, since support for Dreyfus's individual rights also entailed a kind of solidarity with all oppressed Jews. Yet now this element was brought to the forefront. The *anomie* enkindled by the increasing differentiation and isolation of modern life began to transform overt demands for freedom into vehicles for suppressed communal yearnings. Increasingly, protests on behalf of rights were becoming strategies for the production of identity. The nineteenth-century chorus of idiosyncratic intellectuals gathering their voices to affirm our shared principle of rights had metamorphosed into mass demonstrations and ongoing political associations acting in solidarity with whole peoples.

Of course, it couldn't hold. The underlying individualism—

12. This part of Durkheim's argument is set forth in Emile Durkheim, *Suicide* (New York: The Free Press, 1951).

the refusal to be "marshaled"—saw to that. So the mass activism of the 1960s dissipated. Nonetheless, a reformation of the religion of modernity had taken place. Or perhaps we could say that the impulse to communal action in solidarity with whole classes of the oppressed, which had heretofore been concentrated in the European socialist tradition, was now synthesized with a radically individualist version of the dominant liberal political culture of both the United States and Europe. This moral-political synthesis increasingly took the place of traditional religious behavior as the source of meaning in life (when it did not actually reconstitute traditionally religious behavior in its own image). In the decades since, in significant and sometimes hidden ways, the impulse to express solidarity with struggling groups would answer to the need for community within a radically individualist culture.

Why Did the Sixties Happen?

The 1960s grew out of the radical privatization of American life that accompanied suburbanization. Of course, *suburbanization* stands as a kind of shorthand for a complex process, not precisely identical with suburban life. The postwar pattern in which small towns and the old communally organized urban ethnic neighborhoods were broken up into more individualized units has been described by Christopher Lasch and Alan Ehrenhalt.[13] The change was concentrated in suburbs, but as Ehrenhalt has shown, even old urban ethnic enclaves were transformed by the trend toward privatization.

The rise of the postwar suburbs initiated a fraying of the social fabric that, until that time, had knit together communities through bonds of mutual obligation. Now the texture of daily life would be shaped less by neighbors gathered on front stoops than by life

13. Alan Ehrenhalt, *The Lost City* (New York: Basic Books, 1995); Christopher Lasch, *The True and Only Heaven* (New York: W. W. Norton & Co., 1991).

indoors with televisions, transistor radios, records, and the immediate family. And the automobile, that vital suburban accessory
(ownership of which increased exponentially after World War II),
made it possible for people to shop, attend church, and sustain
friendships far outside the confines of their local communities. To
be sure, the shift was never total. Neighborhood friendships and
local civic organizations never entirely disappeared. Increasingly,
however, with the postwar move to the suburbs, friendship and
organizational involvement would be shaped by individual choice,
not by accidents of geography or birth.

This privatization of postwar American life had a double, and
contradictory, effect. On the one hand, we became connoisseurs
of freedom, increasingly sensitive to any diminution in our range
of choice. On the other hand, the collapse of the old social forms
left a yearning to participate in some community of shared moral
purpose. Somehow, we would try to square this circle through a
pattern of temporary participation in a whole range of moral
communities. This *serial communitarianism* would serve as a way
of building up a unique personal identity.

But in what sort of community could a connoisseur of freedom
feel comfortable? Not a traditional community, structured by long-
term networks of sacrifice and support. That sort of community
is built around renunciations—limitations on personal choice. But
what other sort of community is there? Only the one Durkheim
described: a community of individuals collectively taking action
to preserve their liberty. So in the 1960, that is what we got—
movements of individuals who banded together in order to protect
the freedoms cherished by all Americans.

In the process, something was discovered. A collective defense
of liberty could provide the rush of shared purpose and identity
that was increasingly being drained out of our privatized suburban
life. So movements began to coalesce around the theme of resistance to oppression. And as with the early Civil Rights Movement,

there often was much injustice to oppose. Yet now there was a new ingredient. Now the collective defense of liberty and equality would have to shoulder the existential burden once carried by traditional—that is, sacrificial—religion. This invested the process of forming movements of liberation with a special urgency, redoubling the need to find (or create) the all-encompassing threats to life and liberty without which these movements could not survive.

The children of the anomic suburbs reacted convulsively when subjected en masse to the disorienting experience of the move away from home and into college life (the baby boomers entered college in unprecedented numbers). Overtly, these students were asking for more of the same—more of the freedom to which they had been accustomed by suburban living. The rules and restrictions of an old-style education would have to go. The traditional ethic of sacrifice and the practice of sensual self-restraint that went with it was dead—or at least badly wounded. The institutional restraints and sacrificial symbolism of traditional religion made no sense to these kids. To understand Christ on the cross, or Abraham about to kill Isaac, you had to grow up in a family or neighborhood where you regularly relied on others and allowed others to make demands on you. Religious symbolism tells a story about the willingness to give totally of oneself, in trust that the sacrifice will ultimately be redeemed. The kids who still grew up in the neighborhoods based on that sort of mutual obligation and loyalty became the working-class cops who busted the demonstrators' heads for being a bunch of selfish, spoiled brats.

In a sense, the activists of the 1960s simply reproduced, in secular form, the earlier American evangelical movements of social uplift, restoring thereby the sense of collective purpose that had been eroded by suburban life. Yet it would be a mistake to see the crusades of the 1960s as secular in any simple sense. It is not a straightforward question of keeping the social uplift and losing the religious "baggage." The claims of superiority, the group boundaries and rivalries, the determination to impose a monolithic moral narrative on a complex and multivalent world, and even the resolve to govern the most intimate habits and thoughts of the "unreformed" all ended up returning, but this time in a form denuded of the classic, reciprocal ethic of sacrifice. This was, at one and the same time, the oldest story in the book and an honest-to-goodness world-shattering innovation—all the so-called scary concomitants of traditional religious communities, but without the redeeming and unifying sacrificial core. A new core would have to be found.

That new core was to take the form of a collective defense of the individual's sacred rights. Of course, the notion of individual rights had always been central to democracy, yet it coexisted with (and depended upon) the traditional sacrificial ethic. The rights concept dominated our public life while the ethic of sacrifice was the keynote of private life. But now, with the social basis of the old communal forms undermined by suburban privatization, the collective defense of rights increasingly became the religion of those sectors of society released from traditional patterns of mutual obligation and hierarchy.

The Civil Rights Movement of the early 1960s was perhaps the perfect fulfillment of the religion of rights. In that movement, a defense of the sacred rights of the individual generated a deeply felt sense of shared moral purpose across almost every quarter of the nation. But could even this glorious defense of rights serve as the basis for a new way of life? Given the collapse of the old communal forms, it would have to. So by the late 1960s and early 1970s, the notion of rights was sliding into the background of the protests and themes of collective identity (women, blacks, gays, Third World solidarity) moved to the forefront. Of course, manifestly, the demonstrations were concerned with the rights of these groups, but increasingly these gatherings functioned as a new sort of communal affiliation. The loosely knit associational communities that emerged out of these movements were apparently secular, but functioned in many (and often unrecognized) ways like religions. But instead of classic sacrifice, the new religion was centered around images of oppression, of holocaust, of the denial of life or liberty on a mass scale.

In an extraordinary study, Louis Bolce and Gerald De Maio, without quite meaning to do so, trace the rise of the new religion and establish its role in our cultural and political wars.[14] The title of Bolce and De Maio's article is "Our Secularist Democratic Party." What Bolce and De Maio show is that the popular identification of conservative Christians with the Republican Party is only half of the story of the contemporary relationship between religion and political life—and the least interesting half of the story at that. The real political change since the 1960s is not the presence of conservative Christians in the Republican Party. It is, on the contrary, the rise of secularists within the Democratic Party.

Secularists began to appear as a major force within the Democratic Party at the 1972 Democratic National Convention. Prior to this, elites in both parties were committed to traditional Judeo-Christian teachings on authority, sexual mores, and the family. In 1972, however, more than a third of the delegates to the Democratic National Convention described themselves as atheists or agnostics who seldom attended religious services—this at a time when only about 5 percent of the total population fit that description. That faction within the party supported a 1960s-inflected agenda on such issues as abortion, alternative life styles, and the organization of the family. In short, Bolce and De Maio show that the outbreak of our culture war has less to do with a political shift within Christianity than with the rise of secular progressivism within the Democratic Party.

That progressivism may be secular by traditional definitions,

14. Louis Bolce and Gerald De Maio, "Our Secularist Democratic Party," *The Public Interest* (fall 2002), 3–21.

but it is best understood as a new and in important ways illiberal religion, derived from a new social setting, which fulfills a social-moral function in the lives of its adherents analogous to that performed by traditional religion for others. Social scientists have long quarreled over how to define religion.[15] So-called essentialist definitions isolate a core characteristic that everywhere indicates the presence of religion. Most essentialist definitions of religion, of course, identify the phenomenon with the belief in a deity, deities, or other spiritual beings. Functionalist definitions of religion, on the other hand, identify religions by the role that they play in society. Functionalists tend to call any scheme of ideas that answers the fundamental questions about life while offering a template for collective moral action, a religion. Durkheim himself was the first great functionalist student of religion, and I have laid out here a version of Durkheim's claim that the religion of modernity is built around the notion of individual rights.

Once individual rights turn into a religion, liberalism is subverted. Eventually, we are presented instead with a series of Holocaust metaphors, images of mass-scale violations of rights that serve as a charter for collective identity and action. Holocaust metaphors restore the traditional religious notion of radical good and evil and produce political correctness where once there was liberal tolerance. The entire process is rooted in a deep, yet incomplete, transformation of our society in the direction of individualism (and the consequent, if often hidden, effort to overcome atomization through collective political action). The inevitably incomplete nature of modern individualism (no society can sur-

---

15. For an "essentialist" definition of religion, see Melford Spiro, "Religion: Problems of Definition and Explanation," in *Anthropological Approaches to the Study of Religion*, ed. Michael Banton (London: Tavistock, 1966). For a contrasting "functionalist" definition, see Clifford Geertz, "Religion As a Cultural System," in Clifford Geertz, *The Interpretation of Cultures* (New York: Basic Books, 1973).

vive in a totally atomized state) means that the new "secular" religion will never gain total cultural control. On the other hand, without a widespread restoration of traditional communal structures, Holocaust metaphors and the religion of rights will remain powerful. All of this means that for the foreseeable future, we are in for a long and inconclusive culture war. And that war is best understood as a conflict not only between religion and secularism, but between two competing religions.

PART II

POLICY IMPLICATIONS

THREE

Civic
Associations

DAVID DAVENPORT

HANNA SKANDERA

Civic associations play a distinctive and vital role in a democratic
society, developing core virtues and values that enable individuals
to contribute to public life and maintain the political institutions
of a free society. When the young French philosopher Alexis de
Tocqueville visited the United States in the early 1800s, he observed
that democracy in America had been especially strengthened by
broad participation in a wide range of civic associations, including
clubs, churches, nonprofits, and community groups of all types.[1]

1. Alexis de Tocqueville, *Democracy in America*, ed. Harvey C. Mansfield
and Delba Winthrop (Chicago: University of Chicago Press, 2000), 489. This
pattern of American engagement continues. "In 1997, a nationwide poll con-
ducted by the American Association of Retired Persons found that the average
American belongs to 4.2 voluntary groups. Two years earlier, an Independent
Sector study found that almost 70 percent of American households made charitable contributions annually and that just short of half of the population vol-
unteered. Furthermore, those who did volunteer work in 1995 said that they
gave an average of four hours of their time every week." Moreover, Americans'

Even today, leaders of emerging democracies understand that civic associations, and the qualities of mind and character that they encourage, are an essential part of the infrastructure of a thriving free society.[2]

In the last decade, however, scholars have expressed concerns about whether civic associations in America have been altered or weakened. Two major national studies have examined the problem, calling for a renewal of civic engagement and voluntary associations.[3] Some wonder whether old forms of civic association are giving way to new and different ones.[4]

In the context of these debates, this chapter explores a specific question: How has public policy affected the capacity of civic associations to foster the qualities of mind and character that sustain democracy in America ? This requires an appreciation of the historic relationship of three topics: civic associations, which are the independent and voluntary associations of civic life; public policy, which is the collective actions of government, political parties, and other actors that influence the policy sphere; and the virtues and values we recognize as crucial to self-government. These three variables have changed over time and continue to undergo important transformations today.

---

involvement in civic associations remains comparatively strong in relation to other industrialized nations. According to the 1990–91 World Values Survey, only Iceland, Sweden, and the Netherlands citizen involvement is rated ahead of the United States. The National Commission on Civic Renewal, "Civil Society: Evidence—The Condition of Civil Society," *A Nation of Spectators: How Civic Disengagement Weakens America and What We Can Do About It* (College Park: University of Maryland, The National Commission on Civic Renewal, June 1998), available online at http://www.puaf.umd.edu/Affiliates/Civi...eport/table_of_contentsfinal_report.htm.

2. Jeane Bethke Elshtain, "Will the Real Civil Society Advocates Please Stand Up?" *Chicago-Kent Law Review* 75 (2000): 583.

3. See note 9, below.

4. See text at notes 10 and 11, below.

The Historic Formulation

Civic associations in America are a critical source of social capital, or those "features of social organization such as networks, norms, and social trust that facilitate coordination and cooperation for mutual benefit."[5] Many associations, such as churches, synagogues, mosques, scouting organizations, and the like, hold the moral, ethical, and spiritual development of their members as a primary mission. In other cases, nonprofit groups have been organized to promote a particular set of moral principles or goods within government and society, such as human or civil rights. Moreover, civic associations can serve as a kind of buffer or intermediary between individuals and public institutions. They provide citizens with an opportunity to give freely and generously, beyond both the obligations of law and the market's narrower interest in profit.

Alexis de Tocqueville was particularly impressed by the inclination of Americans to form civic associations:

> Americans of all ages, all conditions, all minds constantly unite. Not only do they have commercial and industrial associations in which all take part, but they also have a thousand other kinds: religious, moral, grave, futile, very general and very particular, immense and very small. . . . There is nothing . . . that deserves more to attract our regard than the intellectual and moral associations of America.[6]

Tocqueville thought that the "art of association" was critical because it counteracted wayward democratic tendencies, provid-

---

5. See Robert D. Putnam, "Bowling Alone," *Journal of Democracy* (January 1995): 67. According to Putnam, "the term *social capital* itself turns out to have been independently invented at least six times over the twentieth century, each time to call attention to the ways in which our lives are made more productive by social ties. The first known use of the concept was not by some cloistered theoretician, but by a practical reformer of the Progressive Era—L. J. Hanifan, state supervisor of rural schools in West Virginia" (Putnam, 19).

6. Tocqueville, 489–92.

ing critical lessons in discipline and cooperation.[7] Association thus contributes to that moral virtue among citizens—including respect for others, self-restraint, public spiritedness, and the willingness and ability to participate in the give and take of self-government—that *The Federalist* argues democracy depends upon to a particularly high degree.[8]

Recent Questions About Civic Associations and Values

In recent years, Tocquevillian optimism about America's civic associations has given way to a sense of despair. Alarmed by the apparent decline in civic engagement, two commissions have issued special reports in the past decade. The titles of these reports illustrate some of the problems: *A Nation of Spectators: How Civic Disengagement Weakens America and What We Can Do About It* and *A Call to Civil Society: Why Democracy Needs Moral Truths*.[9]

Robert Putnam's *Bowling Alone* launched a major debate about whether civic associations are in a period of significant decline in

7. Tocqueville, 491, 492, 497.

8. Hamilton, Madison, and Jay, *The Federalist 55*, ed. Clinton Rossiter (New York: New American, a division of Penguin Putnam, Inc., 1999), 314.

9. The National Commission on Civic Renewal, *A Nation of Spectators: How Civic Disengagement Weakens America and What We Can Do About It* (College Park: University of Maryland, The National Commission on Civic Renewal, June 1998), available online at http://www.puaf/umd.edu/Affiliates/Civi...eport/table_of_contentsfinal_report.htm; The National Commission on Civic Renewal, *Update to* A Nation of Spectators *Report* (College Park: University of Maryland, The National Commission on Civic Renewal, September 1999), available online at http://www.puaf/umd.edu/Affiliates/Civi...inalreport/americas_civic_condition.htm; The Council on Civil Society, *A Call to Civil Society, Why Democracy Needs Moral Truths* (New York: Institute for American Values, 1998). According to *A Nation of Spectators: How Civic Disengagement Weakens America and What We Can Do About It*, "America's civic health fell by more than 20 percent between 1984 and 1994. However, the latest statistics show a very significant improvement for 1997."

America, and if so, why. Putnam argues that throughout American history, civic engagement has a record of ups and downs, of renewal and collapse.[10] Pointing to large declines in membership and participation of traditional groups such as the Elks, the PTA, and bowling leagues, he finds that America today is in a period where the pendulum has shifted away from community and toward the individual. Even newer organizations that have arisen are dismissed by Putnam as passive associations in which people participate only by joining and writing a check.[11]

Not everyone agrees with Putnam's reading of the data. According to Francis Fukuyama, "It is not clear that either the number of groups or group memberships in civil society declined overall in this period as the political scientist Robert Putnam has suggested."[12] While acknowledging that certain associations have declined, Putnam's critics point out that this may simply reflect a failure of old groups to innovate and keep up with changes in society, especially the greater spirit of inclusivism in America today. Local associations such as the Elks Club are giving way to mass-

10. Robert D. Putnam, *Bowling Alone* (New York: Simon and Schuster, 2000), 25.

11. Ibid., 49–52; see also Paul Rich, *The Annals, Civil Society, and Democratization*, vol. 565 (1999), 24.

12. Francis Fukuyama, *The Great Disruption* (New York: Free Press, 1999), 60, 71. In a similar vein, ". . . there is no evidence that the average rate of membership has increased in the last quarter-century. This is a surprise because it is widely believed that rising levels of education are linked to greater associational activity. In fact, it appears that two trends over the past quarter-century have roughly counterbalanced each other: The proportion of high school and college graduates in the population has grown larger, but civic participation at every educational level has declined. People with high school diplomas but no college education have become about 32 percent less likely to join any associations, while there has been a modest increase in the proportion of people who belong to no organizations at all." The National Commission on Civic Renewal, *A Nation of Spectators: How Civic Disengagement Weakens America and What We Can Do About It* (College Park: University of Maryland, The National Commission on Civic Renewal, June 1998).

membership organizations like the National Organization for Women and the American Association of Retired Persons. Whether these shifts result in less civic involvement or civic involvement of a lesser quality continues to be a matter for debate.

To answer these questions it is necessary to examine the changing character of civic associations in America. One dramatic change concerns the relation of civic associations to government. Instead of maintaining independence from government, a host of new associations has been born that essentially responds to a more active federal social agenda by seeking to serve it.

1945–1990: Increasing Government
Influence over Civic Associations

Civic associations do not operate in a political vacuum. As much as they might like to be independent of government control and influence, civic associations have been very much subject to the political trends of the larger society as well as to several forms of government oversight. The period following World War II and the Great Society era of the 1960s, for example, saw large expansions of domestic and social programs in America, with a concomitant shift in the role of civic associations and in their dependence upon government. Likewise, the slowdown in federal social programs in the Reagan years had a major influence on civic associations, in both predictable and unexpected ways.[13]

13. While voluntary associations have always been a part of America's fabric, the sheer growth in number of associations over the last thirty-plus years speaks volumes and accentuates their influential status. In 1968, for example, the number of nonprofit organizations of national scope listed in the *Encyclopedia of Associations* totaled 10,200; in 2001, more than 22,000 national organizations were listed and more than 115,000 U.S. associations were identified with interstate, state, intrastate, city, or local scope or membership (Encyclopedia of Associations at http://library.dialog.com/bluesheets/html/bl0114.html). In addition, according to Stephen Macedo in "Constituting Civil Society: School Vouchers, Religious Nonprofit Organizations, and Liberal Public Values" (*Chicago Kent*

Two of the most important ways in which public policy influ-enced civic associations were legislated funding and attempts to regulate and control their membership. Membership defines an association and funding provides for its very existence. Indeed, the purpose of a civic association is often rooted in the origin of its financial support. Not surprisingly, then, the story of voluntary associations from 1945 to 1990 largely parallels federal spending patterns and government funding for nonprofits. Another impor-tant feature of this period is civil rights legislation and resulting court efforts to control the membership of voluntary associations.

Federal Funding and Unhealthy
Dependence on Government

The period following World War II saw a dramatic change in the government-nonprofit relationship and the role of voluntary asso-ciations in society. The historic reluctance of the federal govern-ment to fund private organizations and the resistance of these associations to accepting public monies began to fade. During this postwar period, the federal government undertook a diversifica-tion of its own social agenda, launching new grant programs in education, social welfare (specifically, child welfare), and mental and public health.[14]

Indirect federal support for nonprofit associations rose dra-matically. For example, the 1946 Hospital Survey and Construc-tion Act, commonly known as the Hill-Burton Act, provided nonprofits with capital funding. More than $4.6 billion in Hill-Burton grant funds and $1.5 billion in loans have aided nearly

Law Review 75 [2000], 417, 442–43), there are 1.4 million nonprofit associations in the United States with total income estimated at nearly $320 billion. Of the American workforce, 11 percent are employed in this sector.

14. Waldemar A. Nielsen, *The Endangered Sector* (New York: Columbia Uni-versity Press, 1979), 12–18.

6,800 health-care facilities in more than 4,000 communities since enactment.[15] The federal government also offered technical assistance to nonprofit organizations, as well as state and local governments, to reform and upgrade their programs and improve regulations and standards for health and welfare services. These were sweeping changes from the limited prewar government funding that aided nonprofit organizations.[16]

Even with greatly increased federal support, most nonprofit associations throughout the 1950s remained dependent upon private donations, endowment income, and fees and continued to see themselves as separate from the public sector. Generally, communities responded to social needs through an infusion of public funds, augmented by a specialized response from private associations.[17]

Nevertheless, both public and private social services in the late 1950s and early 1960s met with significant criticism. Activists charged that local hospitals, schools, and volunteer service associations were inefficient, unprofessional, and dehumanizing institutions. Furthermore, they accused private service agencies of having backward social attitudes, neglecting the poor and minorities in favor of the wealthy and middle class, and depriving residents of basic human rights.[18]

By the 1960s, the political climate had become conducive to a major expansion of the federal role in social programs, especially

15. The Hill-Burton Free Care Program, U.S. Department of Health and Human Services at http://www.hrsa.gov/osp/dfcr/about/aboutdiv.htm.

16. Steven Rathgeb Smith, *Civic Infrastructure in America: Government and the Nonprofit Sector*, Report from the Institute for Philosophy and Public Policy (summer 1998) at *http://www.puaf.umd.edu/IPPP/summer1998/civic_infra structure_in_america.htm*.

17. See Nielsen, *The Endangered Sector*.

18. Don Eberly, "The Civil Society Debate: Developments and Prospects, an Institute for American Values Working Paper for the Convening Committee for the Council on Civil Society," Institute for American Values, Publication No. W.P. 53 (New York City: Institute for American Values, 1996), 22.

to President Lyndon Johnson's "Great Society" agenda, with its "war on poverty," major civil rights legislation, and new domestic priorities. Voluntary organizations began providing services that were, for the most part, unavailable prior to the 1960s. Examples include the Economic Opportunity Act, Head Start, the Elementary and Secondary Education Act, community residential programs for the developmentally disabled, outpatient services for the mentally ill, home care, shelters for domestic violence victims, and innovative programs for abused children. In addition, these new federal initiatives encouraged the growth of national advocacy organizations that, in turn, pressed for more funding of nonprofit service agencies.[19]

Public funding also caused these civic and nonprofit associations to focus increasing attention on government and public policy. The cultivation of private support and local community ties became secondary or, in some cases, unnecessary. Federal support diminished the pressure for local fund-raising, further limiting nonprofit efforts in building volunteer networks. Once established, these associations tended to protect their existing service niche rather than create ongoing networks of cooperation among public and private service agencies. Ironically, the very strength of these civic associations—their grassroots volunteerism—gave way to professional staffing and the pursuit and management of government grants.[20] In his case study of public sector politics, Samuel Beer observed:

19. "The Great Society" at *http://www.pbs.org/johngardner/chapters/4c.html*; Smith, *Civic Infrastructure in America*.

20. Steven Rathgeb Smith and Michael Lipsky, *Nonprofits for Hire, the Welfare State in the Age of Contracting* (Massachusetts: President and Fellows of Harvard College, 1993), 9; Timothy Conlan, *From New Federalism to Devolution* (Washington, D.C.: The Brookings Institution, 1998), 158; Kevin M. Brown et al., *Rhetorics of Welfare* (New York: St. Martin's Press, 2000), 4; Smith, note 17 above; Nielsen, *The Endangered Sector*. In the late 1970s, 95 percent of the budget of

> The Great Society acquired a special character by its emphasis
> upon spending for services provided largely by state and local
> governments. . . . To a pronounced degree, there was a profes-
> sionalization of reform. . . . The new programs drew heavily
> upon specialized and technical knowledge in and around the
> federal bureaucracy [and] enhanced [the] importance of scien-
> tifically and professionally trained civil servants at all levels of
> government.[21]

The growth in federal social spending slowed dramatically in
the late 1970s as "the welfare state" in the United States and other
advanced industrial nations was called into question.[22] These concerns contributed to Ronald Reagan's victory in the 1980 presi-
dential election, providing him the opportunity on June 26, 1981,
to enact the Omnibus Budget Reconciliation Act (OBRA). Following the Gramm-Latta II amendment, OBRA established nine new
or revised block grants, consolidating or eliminating 139 categor-
ical programs. This represented the first major wave of devolution
of federal power to state and local governments. Not only were the
number of federal aid programs reduced and consolidated into

---

the Federation of Jewish Philanthropies in New York City was derived from the
government. Nielsen, *The Endangered Sector*, 18.

21. Samuel Beer, "The Adoption of General Revenue Sharing: A Case Study
in Public Sector Politics," *Public Policy* 24 (spring 1976), 160, 162.

22. Federal social welfare expenditures between 1950 and 1980 increased
dramatically: Using a constant, official definition and constant dollars as the
basis of comparison, health and medical costs were 6 times what they were in
1950; public assistance, 13 times; education costs, 24 times their cost in 1950;
social insurance, 27 times; and housing, 129 times their cost (Charles Murray,
Losing Ground [New York: Basic Books, 1994], 14). In the mid-1970s, the total
outlays of private nonprofit organizations, excluding churches, were approxi-
mately $80 billion; $25 billion from private gifts and philanthropy; $23 billion
from government grants, contracts, and purchases of goods and services; and
$32 billion from fees, service charges, and endowment income (*Giving in Amer-
ica: Toward a Stronger Voluntary Sector*, Report of the Commission on Private
Philanthropy and Public Needs [1975], 14).

block grants administered outside of Washington, D.C., but also funds for the programs were decreased by 25 percent.[23]

Paradoxically, the selected cuts in the public sector—and the simultaneous demand for greater accountability for the expenditure of public funds—created many new opportunities for nonprofits, even as they imposed certain constraints and hard choices. States closed public facilities and transferred responsibilities to nonprofit agencies. Some states shifted the management of services such as child welfare and mental health to third-party, nonprofit (and, in some cases, for-profit) organizations. In response, many agencies adjusted their fund-raising strategies, increased fees, and partnered with for-profit organizations. In addition, they often absorbed losses in revenue with lower salaries, longer queues for service, and fewer personnel.[24]

The Reagan cuts and devolution policies also created political ferment, prompting many groups to organize and to petition the government. Some of these organizations sought direct funding, but many were issue-oriented in nature and simply wanted to influence government policy. Overall, the competition for public and private funds increased sharply during this period because the number of nonprofit associations outstripped available resources. The increased competition for both public and private funds discouraged active cooperation among nonprofits and civic associations. Indeed, the fact that government funding for nonprofits had become a paramount concern itself constituted a major shift in the relationship between public policy and civic associations.[25]

23. Conlan, *From New Federalism to Devolution*, 149.
24. Smith, *Civic Infrastructure in America*, 17.
25. Nielsen, *The Endangered Sector*, 14–21; Smith and Lipsky, *Nonprofits for Hire*, 10–11.

Anti-Discrimination Laws and
Attempts to Regulate Membership

The expansionist Great Society agenda included civil rights legislation that, in turn, was followed by antidiscrimination laws at the
state and local levels. Whether or not originally intended, these
laws became tools by which public policy could regulate the membership of voluntary associations. Of course, the membership of a
particular association largely defines its purposes, values, and
goals. The Girl Scouts, for example, will want to limit their membership to girls, and specifically to girls who are committed to the
traditions and values of the Girl Scouts. A religious charity or
school may wish to hire only employees who are part of their faith
heritage in order to perpetuate their values and continue to make
their distinctive contribution. Requiring such associations to
accept members who do not share their core commitments alters
the values of the organization itself and erodes its distinctive contribution to the values of the larger society.

Historically, clubs and voluntary associations have been free
to select members as they wish. Although the United States Constitution does not mention the right of association specifically, the
right has generally been recognized as an essential complement to
the freedoms of press, speech, assembly, and petition protected by
the First Amendment.[26] Courts have concluded that the freedom
to join with others in pursuing activities of mutual interest is
necessary to make the First Amendment freedoms and guarantees
"fully meaningful."

Beginning in 1984 with the case of *Roberts v. Jaycees*,[27] however,
the U.S. Supreme Court began to codify a series of limitations on
the membership rights of civic associations. In that case, the all-

26. Nancy L. Rosenblum, *Membership and Morals* (New Jersey: Princeton
University Press, 1998), 6.
27. 468 U.S. 609 (1984).

male Jaycees sued Minnesota, claiming that the state's Human Rights Act, which prohibited discrimination on the basis of sex in "places of public accommodation," violated their freedom of association. The U.S. Supreme Court disagreed, finding that Minnesota could require the Jaycees to admit women.

Rather than confirm a broad constitutional right to free association, the Court in *Roberts* identified two limited associational freedoms protected by the Constitution: freedom of "intimate association" and freedom of "expressive association." Intimate association is recognized as a "fundamental liberty" but its scope is quite narrow, including only relationships "that attend the creation and sustenance of a family-marriage; the raising and education of children; and cohabitation with one's relatives."[28] Such family relationships would not include a broad organization like the Jaycees. Expressive association involves the exercise of free speech and related First Amendment rights. In this case, however, the Court concluded that the presence of women as members would not alter the message the Jaycees sought to communicate.[29]

Subsequent Supreme Court cases have continued to apply these same limits to the membership rights of civic associations. In *Board of Directors of Rotary International v. Rotary Club of Duarte* (1987),[30] the Court similarly held that the Unruh Act in California did not unconstitutionally forbid the exclusion of women because Rotary Clubs are neither intimate nor expressive associations. Sometimes the Court seems to go out of its way to avoid the associational issues altogether. In the recent case of *Good News Club v. Milford Central School* (2001),[31] it held that a public school could not constitutionally open its facilities to other after-school clubs and programs while excluding a Christian club from

28. Ibid., 619.
29. Ibid., 627–28.
30. 481 U.S. 537 (1987).
31. 533 U.S. 98 (2001).

meeting. The Court's reasoning, however, was based strictly on freedom of speech considerations; indeed, freedom of association is not even mentioned.

A case involving membership rights of the Boy Scouts is often cited as upholding the right of civic associations to limit their membership, but even here the Supreme Court did not find a broader freedom of association, but rather concluded that the Boy Scouts' position on membership qualified as protected "expressive association." In *Boy Scouts of America v. Dale* (2000),[32] the Court found that the application of New Jersey's public accommodation statute to require homosexual membership in the Scouts violated the First Amendment right of expressive association. The Court elaborated on the nature of expressive associations, noting that they need not be advocacy groups but must engage in "some form of expression, whether it be public or private."[33] By attempting to instill certain values in its members, the Scouts were deemed to be engaged in expressive activity. With Scout values such as "morally straight" and "clean" expressed in the Scout Oath and Law, the Court upheld the Scouts' position that homosexuality was inconsistent with their principles.[34]

These membership cases are troublesome in several respects. For one thing, they undervalue the purely associational aspects of voluntary organizations, emphasizing heavily the speech and expression components. While courts have focused on the speech element of associations, the rights of assembly and petition would seem to provide equally valid bases for protecting associations. Associations do important things other than speak. Merely by coming together they may form opinions, exercise influence and have a favorable impact on public life, which courts have not adequately acknowledged. Even the wording of the First Amend-

32. 530 U.S. 640 (2000).
33. Ibid., 648.
34. Ibid., 649–50.

ment—that Congress may make no law abridging the freedom of speech, the freedom of the press, or the right of assembly and petition—implies that all of these rights are fundamental and that Congress should be cautious when it seeks to regulate them.

These cases also undervalue the importance of allowing civic associations to control their membership. As one observer recently noted:

> A large body of research in the social sciences demonstrates that the ability of high social capital groups to choose their own members, free from any compulsion, is often a vital condition for cohesiveness and effectiveness of the groups as well as for the commitment of members to the group and their trust in each other. . . . [W]hen the government interferes with the selection of an association's members, the group's social capital often diminishes as a result.[35]

Unless failure to achieve membership in a particular organization denotes some kind of second-class citizenship, the interest of voluntary associations to control their membership policies should prevail.[36] Indeed, if groups are not able to maintain some cohesiveness of membership, they are unlikely to agree on a set of values or foster any virtues. And they will not find their voices for free expression without such membership control.

In this area, it would seem that public policy is making the same mistake it has made elsewhere on diversity issues. Rather than allowing for a diversity of different kinds of associations—or educational institutions, for example—government seeks to require a diversity of members within each individual association.[37] This tends to dissipate the distinctive values and voice of each

35. Jason Mazzone, "Freedom's Associations," *Washington Law Review* 77 (2002), 639, 762–63.

36. Rosenblum, *Membership and Morals*, 112.

37. Michael W. McConnell, "The New Establishmentarianism," *Chicago Kent Law Review* 75 (2000), 453, 466.

association in favor of a kind of uniformity of association. There should be room in associational life, however, for "bonding" associations, where people of similar backgrounds and interests may assemble, as well as for the "bridging" groups that reach across different types of membership.

Other Governmental Impacts on Civic Associations

In addition to these larger effects on funding and membership, federal policy and legislation has had some indirect, and perhaps even inadvertent, effects on civic associations. For example, although nonprofits are not subject to taxes, tax laws have had an inhibiting effect upon these organizations. In some cases, tax laws have been used as a tool to justify regulation of membership. In other cases, nonprofits have been limited in the scope of their work by claims that some of their programs constitute unrelated business income and are therefore subject to taxation.

Property and zoning laws influence civic associations. In recent years, Congress has passed laws specifically protecting religious associations from governmental interference in their use of land. Even basic laws like the Americans With Disabilities Act may have a dramatic effect on civic associations, requiring them to make expensive accommodations. In many cases, these organizations do not have sufficient funding to meet all the requirements that government may impose.

With increasingly large professional staffs, civic associations must heed employment laws at all levels. Not only their membership but also the ability of civic associations to enjoy preferences in hiring has been affected by antidiscrimination laws and court decisions. Numerous cases raise the question of whether religiously affiliated civic associations may prefer members of their faith group in hiring.[38]

In sum, government limits civic associations in many indirect ways, "imposing regulations, meting out benefits like unemployment insurance, and acting in its ever-expanding capacities as proprietor, employer, educator, and patron."[39] This creates an unfortunate climate in which civic associations are excessively hemmed in by the very entity which, in a healthy democracy, they are supposed to check. As one legal expert put it, "To remain free of regulation, civil society's institutions must remain in government's good graces. On the whole, they must rely on government's willingness to refrain from regulating rather than being assured by constitutional law that government cannot regulate them."[40]

A New Model

Throughout the period of 1945 to 1990, civic associations adopted a new outlook on government. These previously independent, voluntary, grassroots associations began to look more and more to government for their funding and consequently their mission. At the same time, an increasingly active legislative agenda and a flood of litigation have combined to further limit the independence of civic associations. As Amitai Etzioni has said, "the enemy of the civil society . . . is the overbearing state."[41] During this period, state

38. See *Corporation of Presiding Bishops v. Amos*, 483 U.S. 327 (1987) and *EEOC v. Kamehameha*, 990 F.2d 458 (9th Cir. 1993). Compare *McClure v. Salvation Army*, 460 F.2d 553 (5th Cir. 1972), with *EEOC v. Pacific Press*, 990 F.2d 458 (9th Cir. 1993).

39. Rosenblum, *Membership and Morals*, 87.

40. Mark Tushnet, "The Constitution of Civil Society," *Chicago Kent Law Review* 75 (2000), 379, 392–93.

41. Amitai Etzioni, "Law in Civil Society, Good Society and the Prescriptive State," *Chicago Kent Law Review* 75 (2000), 355–56.

regulation has been overbearing and state funding has been seductive.

As a result of the focus of civic associations on government, a second model of the relationship among civic associations, public policy, and values has developed. The traditional model—in which civic associations, rooted in family and community values, both fashioned and checked public policy—still exists. But the huge growth of new associations as well as the restructuring of some of the old ones means that government is now actively shaping the direction of civil society.

Instead of civic associations acting as a check or balance on the state, they are more frequently instruments carrying out government's agenda. In this new model, nearly the reverse of the old, government is acting in a top-down fashion to determine the agenda of civic associations, rather than association members operating from the bottom-up to shape public policy. The driving force has often become funding availability and not membership. In light of these new realities, the ability of voluntary associations to create a distinctive environment, to pursue an independent agenda, and to make their distinctive contribution to democracy in America inevitably declines.

1990–Present:
In Transition to Yet Another Model

The past decades have witnessed continued change in the relationship between public policy and civic associations. Each president has sought to mold the model that emerged in the postwar period. At the same time, a new type of civic association has developed that takes as its primary agenda item influencing public policy and government on a specific issue. There is reason to worry that these changes will further erode the capacity of civic associations to provide ballast against instabilities of democratic political life.

President George H. W. Bush inherited the Reagan slowdown in social spending and devolution of programs from the federal government. Yet he seemed to have a slightly different vision of how this should be carried out. During the campaign, he spoke of a vision for government that was "kinder and gentler." As president, he talked of seeing "a thousand points of light," including both individuals and civic associations that were actively reaching out to help those in need. Bush not only recognized civic associations with awards, but also used the bully pulpit of the presidency to encourage citizens and groups to work together to help fellow citizens in ways that government, alone, could not.

Acknowledging at one point that "the era of big government is over," President Bill Clinton also sought a place for civic associations in augmenting the federal agenda. The Charitable Choice legislation established a new collaboration between government and faith-based organizations. The original Charitable Choice authorization was part of the 1996 federal welfare reform law, and it has now been attached to numerous federal spending programs. Charitable Choice permits religious organizations that receive federal funds to retain their ability to hire on the basis of faith and makes it possible for the government to obtain services from religious organizations.[42]

President George W. Bush has sought to implement an even more proactive relationship between federal programs and civic associations, especially ones that are religiously based. He has established an office of faith-based programs in the White House and has actively pushed a legislative agenda to release what he calls the "armies of compassion" resident in faith-based civic associations. In 2002, the Senate released its version of the president's agenda, the Charity Aid, Recover, and Empowerment Act (CARE),

42. The Center for Public Justice, "Charitable Choice," at *http://www. cpjustice.org/stories/storyReader$277.*

addressing the "unlevel playing field" that faith-based organizations encounter when trying to obtain federal funds. The CARE Act also encourages charitable giving through tax incentives and supports initiatives targeted to "vulnerable" populations. It also sets forth provisions regarding the treatment of nongovernmental providers of social services.[43]

The impact of these developments on citizens' virtues and values is not yet clear. On one hand, bringing additional faith-based organizations into the social services mix would seem likely to increase the ability of civic associations to contribute a diversity of virtue and values, including traditional virtues and values, to public life. In that respect, it could be seen as an effort to strengthen the traditional model. On the other hand, the legislation makes it clear that faith-based organizations may contribute only services, and not their faith, in carrying out government-funded work. That line may be difficult for some associations to observe. And many leaders in the faith-based arena are reluctant to take the federal funding, fearing it may weaken their own values and independence. Clearly, this important redefinition of the relation between civic associations and the state is still being played out.

At the same time, yet another model has emerged. In many quarters, frustration with bureaucracy and nonresponsive policy players has led to the creation of civic associations that have a single-issue, political focus. In effect, these civic associations are formed for the purpose of influencing government or public policy with regard to one matter, from broader concerns such as campaign finance reform or the creation of an international criminal court to one ballot proposition in a single state. They are so active in governmental processes at all levels that, in order to distinguish

43. White House Office of Faith-Based and Community Initiatives at *http://www.whitehouse.gov/government/fbci/legislation.html.*

them from elected representatives, they have come to be called NGOs, or nongovernmental organizations.

These new kinds of civic associations frequently decline to work through normal political processes. Instead, they form their own organizations and often design their own processes. The ease of entry into this domain is appealing. Whereas the traditional political path of change can be long, arduous, and disillusioning, hamstrung by red tape and watered down by compromise, the new politics of the nonprofit is streamlined. All you need is a cause, a 501(c)(3) organization, a membership list, and a good grant writer. The "cause" often is cloaked in language that meets the requirements for a federal grant. Voilà! The new nonprofit now has direct access in the political process for lobbying, political contributions, sponsoring ballot propositions, and the like.

Consider two examples, one domestic and one international. State ballot propositions have exploded along with these new NGOs. Originally designed as a populist option to allow the people to speak occasionally through direct democracy, ballot initiatives have now become a regular end-run around the legislative process. In California alone, there have been an astonishing 279 ballot propositions in the past 20 years, mostly for issues that the legislature should and normally does consider anyway.[44]

Special interest groups have found it easier to sponsor and pass a ballot proposition than to get legislative action through the normal political processes. It was far easier for actor Arnold Schwarzenegger to form a civic association or nonprofit and get the people to vote in favor of devoting part of California's education budget for after-school programs than to pass such a bill in the state legislature, where there is a huge deficit and priorities must

44. David Davenport, "Proposition Glut," *San Francisco Chronicle* (November 2, 2002).

be balanced and paid for.[45] In 1998, nearly $100 million was spent by Nevada gaming interests, among others, for a ballot proposition about gambling on Indian reservations. The organizations formed to raise money and run advertising for these single-issue propositions exemplify the new model of civic associations.[46]

Similarly, such associations are flexing their political muscle on the international scene. Whereas diplomacy used to be by and between nation-states, NGOs are no longer in the hallways merely advising, rather they are now driving many treaty negotiations. In the recent development of the International Criminal Court, for example, and the Ottawa treaty banning land mines, NGOs played a primary role in establishing a process outside the normal nation-to-nation negotiation, in drafting language, lobbying delegates, and enacting the treaty.[47] Two Canadian political scientists who observed the leadership of NGOs in the development of the land mines treaty observed that the process was "inexplicable in the context of conventional international relations."[48] NGOs active in international affairs have proliferated dramatically, at least quadrupling in the last decade.[49]

What effect does this have on virtues and values? Interestingly, many of these single-issue associations present their case in moral, even moralizing, terms. But the goods are not the broader ones of participation, community spirit, and compromise offered by the traditional civic association, but very narrow ones that support the particular issue at hand. One supporter of the land mines treaty,

45. "Proposition 49," KTVU News at http://www.netelection.org/ktvu/Propositions/Prop49.asp.

46. See David S. Broder, *Democracy Derailed* (New York: Harcourt, 2000).

47. David Davenport, "The New Diplomacy," *Policy Review*, no. 17 (2002), 116.

48. Michael Dolan and Chris Hunt, "Negotiating in the Ottawa Process," *To Walk Without Fear*, ed. Maxwell A. Cameron et al. (New York: Oxford University Press, 1998), 393.

49. Davenport, "The New Diplomacy," 20.

for example, openly described the process used by NGOs as the "mobilization of shame."[50]

Indeed, part of the agenda of these new civic associations is to convert political issues into moral crusades, promoting absolutist positions that polarize the debate.[51] Mainstream political actors generally take their positions based on outcomes, recognizing the need to compromise and find practical solutions. More radical participants, including many of these new NGOs, pursue change because the conduct they seek to regulate is good or bad in itself.[52] The passionate single-issue voice is quite different from the broader role formerly played by civic associations.

Conclusion

The story of civic associations and their relationship to public policy and the qualities of mind and character on which democracy depends parallels the larger themes of this volume. America's founders recognized that the civic virtues developed in what we have been calling civic associations. Alexis de Tocqueville, who saw the consequences of the loss of "core intermediaries" in the French revolution, emphasized the importance of America's taking a different course.[53]

When we shift to the present era, observers report a huge loss of those virtues and values in American public life. Daniel Yankelovich, a member of the Council on Civil Society, observed in 1996 that "public distress about the state of our social morality has reached nearly universal proportions: 87 percent of the public fear

50. Ibid., 21.
51. Raymond Tatalovish and Byron W. Daynes, *The Social Regulatory Process, Moral Controversies in American Politics* (New York: M. E. Sharpe, 1998), 259.
52. Theodore J. Lowi, "Forward," *Moral Controversies in American Politics*, ed. Raymond Tatalovish and Byron W. Daynes (New York: M. E. Sharpe, 1998), XIX.
53. Tocqueville, *Democracy in America*.

that something is fundamentally wrong with America's moral condition," up from 76 percent just a year before. "In general, a widespread feeling of moral decline has sharply expanded within the public over the last two years, regardless of gender, age, race, or geographical area," according to Yankelovich. According to a Gallup Poll, 78 percent of the public rates "the state of moral values in the country" as either very weak or somewhat weak and about 76 percent believe that moral values have deteriorated in the past 25 years.[54] And the report, *A Call to Civil Society: Why Democracy Needs Moral Truths*, concluded by connecting moral decline to the weakening of civic associations: "[O]ur democracy is growing weaker because we are using up but not replenishing the civic and moral resources that make our democracy possible."[55]

As this chapter has argued, however, it may not be only a decline in membership of civic associations but also a change in the relationship among civic associations and the state that requires closer examination. The first model of this relationship—civic associations fostering grassroots values—prevailed until the postwar period. Although not replaced, these traditional associations began, from the 1960s forward, focusing their agenda increasingly on government funding and responding to government regulation. More significantly, during this same period, a second model and a new generation of civic associations arose, one whose role was primarily defined by the carrying out of the government's social agenda. Its values came not from the grassroots level of its members, but from Washington. The vital roles of civic associations as a check on government and as an intermediary between people and government declined.

More recently, a third model of civic associations has appeared, with NGOs forming to influence government policy on specific issues. Although their work is often couched in the language of

54. The Council on Civil Society, *A Call to Civil Society: Why Democracy Needs Moral Truths* (New York: Institute for American Values, 1998).
55. Ibid.

values, these values are quite different. They are not the broad values of participation that make democracy as a whole work, but rather are the narrow values that support a particular point of view on a specific issue. As a result, public policy has become more contentious and less collaborative, and as E. J. Dionne argued in his classic *Why Americans Hate Politics*, this has resulted in great frustration with the political process.[56]

To some degree, the style of this third, more confrontational model fits the nature of the baby-boomer generation that came of age in the 1960s. Studies suggest that the next generation of Americans will be quite different. Surveys show, for example, that today's college students are far less politically active than the baby-boomer generation, a sign to which many point with despair. But what is not much discussed is what this generation finds to be of greater priority: family and community service. When it comes to fostering virtues and values, family and community service (civic associations indirectly) may be the most important contributors.[57] In other words, some of their strength comes from those same grassroots areas that fueled the traditional model of civic associations. With the need so great and the stakes so high, there is reason to press forward and consider public policies that will cultivate or at least not erode the forms of civic association that support democratic self-government.

56. See E. J. Dionne, *Why Americans Hate Politics* (New York: Simon and Schuster, 1991).

57. Higher Education Research Institute at UCLA's Graduate School of Education and Information Studies, "2001 CIRP Press Release: CIRP Freshman Survey" at *http://www.gseis.ucla.edu/heri/01_press_release.htm*; Linda J. Sax, Alexander W. Astin, William S. Korn, and Kathryn M. Mahoney, *The American Freshman: National Norms for Fall 2000* (Los Angeles: Higher Education Research Institute, UCLA, 2000). Results from the "2001 Freshman Survey" recorded all-time high volunteerism rates with 82.6 percent of incoming freshmen reporting frequent or occasional volunteer work, compared with a low of 66 percent in 1989. According to the "2000 Freshman Survey," 72.7 percent ranked "raising a family" as important and only 17.9 percent of freshmen ranked "influencing a political structure" as important.

FOUR

Schooling

CHESTER E. FINN JR.

Every society, from the most primitive to the exquisitely sophis-
ticated, has devised mechanisms for teaching its young what they
must know to enter successfully into that society as adults. This
preparation-and-induction process typically includes the society's
essential skills, rules, and mores as well as the core values that the
culture honors.

In America, as in other advanced countries, this process takes
numerous forms and engages myriad formal institutions and
informal structures. These include family, neighborhood and
church, a host of other civil-society organizations, and—our present focus—the schools.

Schooling in the United States is typically compulsory for ten
to twelve years of a youngster's life, usually from age five or six
through sixteen or seventeen. Further education is widely available
at low cost (to the consumer, at least) for as many more years as
anyone might want. During the compulsory period—essentially
first grade through high school—the main provider is government,

ordinarily in the form of state government operating through local education agencies, underwritten by a mix of state and local tax funding and overlaid by sundry federal programs, regulations, and subsidies.

Relying primarily on government as the chief source of schooling creates an instant paradox when it comes to educating the children of a liberal society in values, virtues, and citizenship. Because we cherish freedom as a core value and insist that the state is the creature of its citizens, we are loath to allow state-run institutions to instruct tomorrow's citizens in how to think, how to conduct themselves, and what to believe. Because a free society is not self-maintaining, however, because its citizens must know something about democracy and individual rights and responsibilities, and because they must also learn how to behave in a law-abiding way that generally conforms to basic societal norms and values, it is the obligation of all educational institutions, including primary and secondary schools, to assist in the transmission of these core ideas, habits, and skills. Indeed, we fret when we learn of schools that *neglect* this role, even private schools. One of the more effective debating points scored against voucher plans, for example, is the allegation that "Klan schools," "witchcraft schools," and "madrasas" (fundamentalist Islamic schools) will qualify for public subsidy even as they impart malign values to their pupils. But should government define which values are sound? A paradox indeed. We want good citizens to emerge from all our schools, yet we don't want schools that operate as arms of the state to dictate their values and virtues. And we don't want privately operated schools to instill the wrong values in them.

Lurking behind that paradox is a darker possibility: that today's schools are not just ambivalent and skittish when it comes to values and virtues and hence are doing a lackluster job of transmitting them to the young, but that these institutions may actually be causing harm in this domain. Some schools and educators are flirting with worrisome values such as moral relativism, atheism, agnosticism toward democracy, excessive deference to the "pluribus" at the expense of the "unum," discomfort with patriotism, cynicism toward established cultural conventions and civic institutions. Transmitting such values to children will, over time, erode the foundations of a free society. We must now contemplate the disturbing possibility that the schools we once counted upon to promote values that support freedom may in fact be doing the opposite.

Schooling in the United States

Like most developed societies, America requires its children to attend school but does not force them to enroll in government-operated schools. That's been clear since the Supreme Court's *Pierce v. Society of Sisters* decision in 1925. "The fundamental theory of liberty upon which all governments in this Union repose," ruled the justices, "excludes any general power of the state to standardize its children by forcing them to accept instruction from public teachers only." At the same time, however, the high court affirmed the state's authority to ensure that all of its children receive an education from acceptable schools—schools that, the justices never doubted, would include the formation of good citizens among their purposes:

> No question is raised concerning the power of the state reason-
> ably to regulate all schools, to inspect, supervise, and examine
> them, their teachers, and pupils; to require that all children of
> proper age attend some school, that teachers shall be of good
> moral character and patriotic disposition, that certain studies
> plainly essential to good citizenship must be taught, and that

nothing be taught which is manifestly inimical to the public welfare.[1]

A debate has raged forever among economists and theoreticians as to whether the benefits of education are predominately public (accruing to the society) or largely private (adding to the prosperity and life prospects of individuals receiving it). That there's no debate victor in sight attests to the fact that the right answer is surely "yes": Education confers both types of benefits, which is also why its control, financing, and delivery are shared between public and private sectors. The Court's *Pierce* decision recognized the balancing of interests that typifies America's approach to primary-secondary schooling whereby, in addition to government schools, families may opt for privately operated schools, home schooling, and, of late, such variants as charter schools, even cyberschools. Many hybrids exist today, and more will exist tomorrow. The options are numerous—but not the option of shunning education altogether. Government does require that all youngsters get some form of schooling and makes its version freely available to all comers, courtesy of the taxpayers, whereas most others charge tuition or fees. No wonder government schooling has captured the lion's share of the education market.

The complexities grow more tangled when we observe that at least three levels of government are engaged in the funding and regulation (and, to a degree, the delivery) of "public" education in America. Primary constitutional responsibility is vested in the fifty states, but they (except for Hawaii) have opted to delegate much of the heavy lifting to local education agencies, which usually (but not always) correspond to town or county borders but which are often independent, in whole or in part, from the mayors, city councils, aldermen, and county commissioners who run the police

---

1. *Pierce v. Society of the Sisters of the Holy Names of Jesus and Mary*, 268 U.S. 510 (1925).

department and ensure that the trash gets collected. About ninety-three cents of the average public school budget dollar come from a blend of state and local tax revenues—a blend that varies greatly from place to place—with Washington contributing the rest. Essential policy decisions—such as who will teach, who is qualified to lead schools, will there be kindergarten, at what age may youngsters leave school, who selects textbooks—are similarly complex, with all three (and sometimes more) levels of government involved. Moreover, the tradition in some parts of the country (for example, Colorado) is for "local control" to predominate in K–12 schooling while in other places (for example, New York), the state sets most of the rules.

When it comes to the *content* of schooling, including both the explicit academic curriculum and the teaching of values and character, it has not been many years since most such decisions were made locally—at the town level, in the principal's office, even in the individual classroom. The states generally discharged their self-imposed education responsibility by enacting and (more or less) enforcing "compulsory attendance" laws and furnishing free public schools wherein those laws could be obeyed. Though school resources and operations were governed by hundreds of laws and regulations, the state said relatively little about what pupils would actually learn in school. Though most states gradually introduced certain academic requirements, for decades these consisted mainly of a student's obligation to earn enough "Carnegie units" to graduate from high school by being able to show on his transcript that he had completed a specified number of courses in designated fields.

With the passage of time, some states went further, mandating particular courses that all pupils must take. (A year of U.S. history during high school was perhaps the most common of these requirements.) And a few jurisdictions grew much more specific. The public schools of California and Texas, for example, could only use (at state expense, anyway) textbooks that state agents had vetted and approved. New York's powerful Board of Regents, via its legendary "Regents exams," spelled out the actual content of particular courses, at least at the secondary level. For the most part, however, curricular decisions still remained in the hands of locally run school systems, individual schools, and teachers. The state had little to say about them, although a high degree of uniformity crept in via professional norms within the education field (for example, the National Council of Teachers of Mathematics' view of middle school math, the International Reading Association's approach to primary reading), ubiquitous college entrance requirements (for example, fluency in a foreign language), the academic priorities of private organizations that administer widely used national tests (for example, the SAT and Advanced Placement exams), and by the remarkably homogeneous thoughtworld (to use E. G. Hirsch's term) that dominates what is taught and learned in the education colleges where most American educators are trained.

The State's Role Grows

During the 1970s, America awakened to the troubling facts that some of its high school graduates could barely read and many were ill-prepared for college and the workforce. One by one, state governments responded by enacting "minimum competency" tests that young people had to pass as part of demonstrating their fitness for a diploma. This had the effect of intruding the state directly into the specification of academic skills that all students must learn—and show that they possessed. It had the further effect of beginning to centralize and standardize such decisions, which previously had been handled in disparate ways by local school boards, even individual teachers.

Nor did the centralizing stop there. After the National Commission on Excellence in Education informed us in 1983 that the nation was at risk due to the weak academic attainments of our students, states and, increasingly, the federal government began to get much more concrete about what pupils must learn at various grade levels. The "excellence movement," as some termed it, evolved into what is now called "standards-based reform," wherein (typically) the state prescribes a body of skills and knowledge that all schools are supposed to teach and all children are supposed to learn; administers tests designed to give everyone feedback on how well those standards are being met; and imposes rewards and sanctions intended to prod children and educators into doing better. Under recent federal law, all states must set academic standards for their public schools in three core subjects; give annual tests to see how well those standards are being attained; and devise "accountability" systems that seek, through a combination of carrots and sticks, to alter the behavior of students, teachers, and schools so as to foster the attainment of these standards. The No Child Left Behind Act (2001) gives every state twelve years to get *all* its students achieving at a "proficient" level vis-à-vis the state's own academic standards.

These standards normally apply to all public schools within state boundaries, including both those run by local school systems and those that operate as charter schools. Rarely, though, do they apply to private schools or home schoolers—yet another accommodation to the awkward, yet quintessentially American, balancing of public and private interests in the education sector. Moreover, the federal requirements bear only on reading, math, and science, deferring to states and communities to shape the remainder of their own standards and curricula. It's common, however, for states to add "social studies" to their standards, and often art and literature, too. Further muddying the waters, even as states set new standards for academic outcomes, a number of old input-style graduation requirements also linger on the statute books, such as the tradition of everyone taking U.S. history in eleventh grade. Also present in many states are curricular prescriptions in health, physical education, home economics, and other subjects that, at some point, a legislature or board of education deemed so important as to mandate for all schools.

Teaching Values, Preparing Citizens

Today's statewide standards may or may not extend explicitly into values education and character formation. Most schools, however, find themselves enmeshed in these domains for several reasons, beginning with the fact that they consider themselves charged with developing good citizens, not just people who can read, write, cipher, get into college, and earn a living. Indeed, when Americans are asked what are the earmarks of a decently educated person at the conclusion of compulsory schooling, most place citizenship high on the list. An overwhelming majority believes that it's "very important" for all schools to prepare young people to be "responsible citizens."[2] Yet we also harbor grave doubts that government should dictate the values, beliefs, attitudes, and behaviors that comprise such citizenship.

How have U.S. schools sought to square this circle? First, when developing standards and curricula in social studies, they generally accompany the traditional disciplinary content of history, geography, economics, and government with some direct attention to citizenship, social norms, and the like. This may or may not include overt "character education," but it nearly always incorporates civic values, rights, responsibilities, and participation, at least in its statement of aspirations. Here, for example, is the opening paragraph of New Jersey's description of its "core curriculum content standards for social studies":

2. Annual Kappan/Gallup survey, including 1996. See note 21, David E. Campbell, for specifics.

Citizen participation in government is essential in forming this nation's democracy and is vital in sustaining it. Social studies education promotes loyalty and love of country, and it prepares students to participate intelligently in public affairs. Its component disciplines foster in students the knowledge and skills needed to make sense of current political and social issues. By studying history, geography, American government and politics, and other nations, students can learn to contribute to national, state and local decision making. They will also develop an understanding of the American constitutional system, an active awareness and commitment to the rights and responsibilities of citizenship, a tolerance for those with whom they disagree, and an understanding of the world beyond the borders of the United States.[3]

The school's formal curriculum is the most obvious place to augment "book learning" with a suitable concern for citizenship. When this succeeds, children come to understand how the government works and what it means to live in a democracy, while also learning how to behave in the public square (obey the traffic laws, pay your taxes, vote, wait your turn for the bus, engage in volunteer work, and so on.)

As one's conception of citizenship expands from understanding to participating, however, the formal curriculum's inherent limits become manifest. For example, a recent report, "The Civic Mission of Schools" by the Carnegie Corporation of New York, offers four goals for civic education, all denominated in terms of "competent and responsible citizens" whose development is the main point. The first of those goals says that such citizens are "informed and thoughtful," which can mesh with a classically curricular view of the school's role. But the other three—"participate in their communities," "act politically," and "have moral and

---

3. State of New Jersey Web site, http://www.state.nj.us/njded/cccs/11soc intro.html.

civic virtues"—are harder to instill through conventional books and teaching.[4]

Some of these subtler and more behavioral civics lessons may be embedded in the pedagogies and classroom methods that are prescribed or assumed in state standards for various subjects, including some that range far beyond social studies and that often carry controversies of their own. These may involve learning "cooperatively" (which critics see as destructive of American individualism, even as fostering socialist ways) and engaging in "critical thinking" (which can be quite upsetting to followers of traditional faith-based religions). Even when such lessons are not spelled out in formal state standards, they are apt to turn up in classrooms and schools because they hew to the pedagogical dispositions of many educators. When they do turn up, unfortunately, we begin both to see disgruntled parents and to glimpse some of the ways that today's schools can end up weakening the base of a free society.

There was a time, primarily in the 1980s, when a number of states poked into students' values and, especially, behavior. Known as "outcomes-based" education, this began as a logical response to the era's new focus on schooling's discernible results rather than simply its inputs and requirements. In some jurisdictions, however, it led to a focus on pupil attitudes and actions, such as "respecting diversity" and "working collaboratively with others." This proved politically untenable—parents protested against government imposing patterns of behavior or thought on children under the guise of mandatory academic standards. So most states pulled back from behavioral and affective standards and confined their standards to the more strictly cognitive domains.

There had been an earlier time, mainly during the 1970s flow-

4. "The Civic Mission of Schools" (New York: Carnegie Corporation of New York and CIRCLE: The Center for Information and Research on Civic Learning and Engagement, February 2003), 10.

ering of postmodernism and relativism on university campuses, when some prominent educators, most famously Harvard professor Lawrence Kohlberg, urged schools to encourage children to "clarify" their own values. Instead of instructing youngsters on which values they should hold, such educators held that their responsibility was to refrain from being "judgmental" and, instead, to elicit the values that presumably lurk within the bosom of every human being. This, too, produced a backlash among parents who felt that teachers should admonish children as to the difference between right and wrong, not refrain from such distinctions. But it left a lasting imprint on the education profession and on the training of teachers and principals.

These episodes suggest the basic problem: When they enter the domain of virtues and values, schools and educators can do harm as well as good by, for example, teaching youngsters that moral judgments are relative, idiosyncratic, and anchored to nothing but one's own opinions or preferences. Yet we also see that schools (and educators) are damned both when they do enter this domain and when they don't. Beyond a very narrow core of civic values, Americans hold strong but often divergent views about the virtues and values they want their children to acquire, about the role of teachers and schools in inculcating those virtues and values, and, especially, about the role of distant governments in trying to shape, standardize, and regulate such decisions.

Signs of Weakness

Our continuing ambivalence about these matters—uncertainty that it's any of the school's business and worry that the formal education system's direct engagement with such sensitive matters may lead to vexed outcomes—helps to explain why many schools have done a lackluster job of instilling values and developing character in youngsters. Certainly there's ample evidence—cheating, violence, and so on—that a lot of youngsters aren't acquiring and internalizing the virtues that most adult Americans think they should espouse and practice. To be sure, some blame for such failings must be laid at the door of negligent and self-absorbed (or absent) parents, the baleful influence of the mass media, and other negative forces at work in the lives of children. Still, responsibility must also be shared by the education profession, which for the most part is awash in relativism, postmodernism, multiculturalism, and childcenteredness, all calculated *not* to produce teachers (or textbooks, lesson plans, and so on) who think it's their job to instruct children on the difference between right and wrong, good and bad, beautiful and ugly, democratic and authoritarian. We know from a recent survey of education-school professors that their own beliefs about what's important for teachers to know and schools to do are distant from those of most ordinary Americans.[5] We also know that teachers, like everyone else, live and learn within a broader culture that transmits insalubrious values (via television, popular music, and so on), even as it signals that anything goes— that one's own pleasures and needs deserve top priority and that well-behaved grown-ups don't render harsh judgments or make invidious comparisons.

Whatever the reasons for their dereliction, the recent Carnegie report blasted the schools for doing a weak job with their "civic mission" and insisted that their doorstep is where this responsibility properly belongs, if only because other institutions "have lost the capacity or will to engage young people. . . . Schools can help reverse this trend."[6]

5. Steve Farkas and Jean Johnson, *Different Drummers: How Teachers of Teachers View Public Education* (New York: Public Agenda, 1997). This was the first comprehensive survey ever undertaken of the views of education professors from United States colleges and universities. Their vision of education and the mission of teacher education programs are explored, including their attitudes toward core curriculum, testing, standards, and the public's parameters.

6. Carnegie, "The Civic Mission of Schools," 5.

Note, though, that disappointment and discontent regarding the public schools' performance in fostering sound values in children are not just a recent story. Confusion and conflict in this domain have deeper roots, beginning with the reality that in a pluralistic society, values that one group deems admirable may be abhorrent to another. As long ago as the 1890s, for example, U.S. Catholic leaders determined that the public schools of their day, more or less overtly Protestant, were a danger to the "faith and morals" of young Catholics. This led to the Church's decision to create the far-flung system of parochial schools that still largely endures today. The defection of many Catholics from the public schools did not, however, cause those schools to become even more Protestant. Instead, they gradually turned more secular, sometimes stridently so, banning even silent prayer and Christmas pageants. That secularism is one reason that most Catholic youngsters today attend public schools. But it also led other parents—especially fundamentalist Christians—to conclude that their own children's faith and morals were in mounting jeopardy, which gave rise to yet another crop of private schools, the fast-spreading network of "Christian schools" of the past quarter-century.

Other groups, many of them defined by religious belief, have created their own private schools, including Quakers, Lutherans, Jews, and, recently, Muslims. This option (combined, of late, with home schooling) has provided a partial solution to the values-in-public-education quandary. So have some of today's charter schools that work especially hard on moral and character education. There is much to be said for such pluralistic developments in terms of character formation, academic progress, and the likelihood that the child's school will reinforce values that are important to his parents. But with every new set of schools devoted to the beliefs of one or another segment of our polyglot population, we also add to the risk of societal fragmentation and to our uncertainty that the values being taught to children in those schools will strengthen the foundations of a liberal democracy.

Obstacles to Improvement

The regular public schools, meanwhile, have become both more secular—surely more secular than the First Amendment requires—and more value-free. The education profession's cherished "progressivism" is part of the reason. And the close scrutiny of fierce watchdog groups that scan the horizon for the slightest hint of religiosity in public schools also has made schools and educators gun-shy. In recent years, however, perhaps the strongest influences have been postmodern relativism and multiculturalism, which first trickled, then gushed from the university campus into primary and secondary school classrooms. If scholars, teachers, and those who train them abjure fixed distinctions between right and wrong, if all judgments are said to depend upon one's unique perspective or background rather than universal standards of truth, beauty, or virtue, if every form of family, society, and polity is deemed equal to all other forms, and if every group's mores and values must be taught (along with its culture, its food, its music, its history, and so on), who is there (in school) to help children determine what it means to be an American, how to behave, and what to believe?

Further complicating this picture is the spread of what we may term the political activism conception of civic education, such as that espoused in the new Carnegie study, which sees influencing public policy and engaging in political activity as the highest—maybe the only legitimate—form of civic participation and which gives short shrift to being a good parent, a dependable neighbor, and a conscientious member of the nongovernmental institutions that comprise civil society. It even faults nonpolitical, school-based "service-learning" programs on the dubious grounds that they may encourage "students to volunteer in place of political participation."[7]

Civic education is also roiled by overwrought political correctness and hypersensitivity to the possibility of textbook bias or controversy. This baleful influence arises on both left and right. As the eminent education historian Diane Ravitch recently noted, "The content of today's textbooks and tests reflects a remarkable convergence of the interests of feminists and multiculturalists on one side and the religious right on the other. No words or illustrations may be used that might offend the former groups, and no topics can be introduced that might offend those on the other side of the ideological divide."[8]

Hence much gets omitted from class materials and much of what remains has been sanitized to the point that it could not possibly offend any person, group, cause, or viewpoint. This has the effect of depriving schools and teachers of a huge fraction of the very stories, books, poems, plays, and legends from which children might best learn the difference between good and evil, right and wrong, hero and villain, patriot and traitor. And because this peculiar paranoia has now been internalized by curriculum writers and textbook publishers, it has the further effect of causing new instructional materials to be value-free from the outset. Escalated to the level of state standards and district curricula, it substitutes mushy generalities for specifics. Nowhere is this clearer than in the troubled subject known as social studies.

The Social Studies Mess

The man in the street probably still supposes that social studies is mainly about history and civics leavened with some geography and

7. Ibid., 26.
8. Diane Ravitch, "Education After the Culture Wars," *Daedalus* (summer 2002), 15. Also see her book, *The Language Police* (New York: Knopf, 2003).

economics and that at the end of a well-taught K–12 social studies sequence, young people will know who Abraham Lincoln and Theodore Roosevelt were, why World War II was fought, how to find Italy and Iraq on a map, what "supply and demand" means, and how many senators each state sends to Washington for terms of what duration.

If that were so, school-based social studies would contribute to the forging of citizens, at least on the cognitive side. But that's not what animates the experts who dominate this field, shape its academic standards and textbooks, and signal to ed-school professors and primary-secondary teachers alike what is important for children to learn.

The main professional organization in this field is the National Council for the Social Studies (NCSS). Here is its view of what schools should accomplish:

> A well-designed social studies curriculum will help each learner construct a blend of personal, academic, pluralist, and global views of the human condition in the following ways: Students should be helped to construct a *personal perspective* that enables them to explore emerging events and persistent or recurring issues, considering implications for self, family, and the whole national and world community. . . .
>
> Students should be helped to construct an *academic perspective* through study and application of social studies learning experiences. The social studies disciplines provide specific points of view. . . . The informed social studies learner applies knowledge and processes from academic disciplines and from interdisciplinary means to both personal and social experiences.
>
> Students should be helped to construct a *pluralist perspective* based on diversity. This perspective involves respect for differences of opinion and preference; of race, religion, and gender; of class and ethnicity; and of culture in general. This construction should be based on the realization that differences exist among individuals and the conviction that this diversity can be positive and socially enriching. . . .

> Students should be helped to construct a *global perspective* that includes knowledge, skills, and commitments needed to live wisely in a world that possesses limited resources and that is characterized by cultural diversity. A global perspective involves viewing the world and its people with understanding and concern. This perspective develops a sense of responsibility for the needs of all people and a commitment to finding just and peaceful solutions to global problems.[9]

As this position statement makes plain, American education has a sizable problem with the field of social studies itself, a field that has become steadily less interested in students' basic knowledge of civics and history and more devoted to their "perspectives" and choices. This problem was underscored in the curricular guidance that the NCSS and many other education groups provided to teachers with respect to lessons about the horrific terrorist attacks on the United States on September 11, 2001, and their anniversary a year later. Such guidance encouraged teachers to deal with students' feelings about those events, to help them feel good about themselves, to be nice, tolerant, and multicultural, but not really to teach them who attacked America and why our values are despised or feared (or envied) by some of the world's inhabitants.[10]

If "reformers" such as the Carnegie group have their way, however, the NCSS will have even more clout and civic education will be slanted even more in the direction of its political values—and away from the kinds of book-learning that may at least ground children in important information. (The Carnegie report itself is schizophrenic about knowledge, first admonishing schools to do better at instructing students in "government, history, law, and democracy," then deprecating "rote facts" on grounds that these

9. National Council for Social Studies Web site, http://www.social studies.org/standards/1.2.html.

10. For a fuller discussion of the problems with 9/11 curriculum guidance and for an alternative body of guidance organized by the Thomas B. Fordham Foundation, see *http://www.edexcellence.net/Sept11/September11.html*.

"may actually alienate [pupils] from politics.") Thus, we face a truly perplexing problem: Our schools have not done well at forging character, values, or civic consciousness in young Americans. They may, in fact, be teaching harmful lessons that will weaken the foundations of a free society and sap its willingness to trumpet its core principles and defend its vital interests. Meanwhile, they have failed even to impart specific information to children about their country's history and how its government and civil institutions work. That is why many studies document the thinness of student knowledge of basic civics and history. The federally funded testing program called the National Assessment of Educational Progress (NAEP) is a recurrent source of such evidence.

Here, for example, is the NAEP Governing Board's description of what it means for students to be "proficient" in civics at the twelfth-grade level:

> Twelfth-grade students performing at the *Proficient* level should have a good understanding of how constitutions can limit the power of government and support the rule of law. They should be able to distinguish between parliamentary systems of government and those based on separate and shared powers, and they should be able to describe the structure and functions of American government. These students should be able to identify issues in which fundamental democratic values and principles are in conflict—liberty and equality, individual rights and the common good, and majority rule and minority rights, for example, and they should be able to take and defend positions on these issues. They should be able to evaluate ways that law protects individual rights and promotes the common good in American society. They should understand how the application of fundamental principles of American constitutional democracy has expanded participation in public life, and they should be able to explain how citizens can work individually and collectively to monitor and influence public policy. These students should understand the importance and means of participation in political life at the national, state, and local levels. They should be

able to evaluate contributions made by political parties, interest groups, and the media to the development of public policy, and they should be able to explain how public service and political leadership contribute to American democracy. They should understand how American foreign policy is made and carried out, and they should be able to evaluate the performance of major international organizations. Finally, these students should be able to discuss reasons for and consequences of conflicts that arise when international disputes cannot be resolved peacefully.[11]

That's an exemplary summary of the knowledge and understanding of civics that many Americans want the schools to impart to their children. In 1998, however, just 26 percent of high school seniors attained that level of success on the NAEP civics assessment. Three-quarters fared worse, including large fractions who scored far below that level.

United States history also presents a bleak picture. This vital subject was most recently assessed in 2001, and once again a chasm yawned between the desirable and the actual. According to the NAEP Governing Board,

Twelfth-grade students performing at the *Proficient* level should understand particular people, places, events, ideas, and documents in historical context, with some awareness of the political, economic, geographic, social, religious, technological, and ideological factors that shape historical settings. They should be able to communicate reasoned interpretations of past events, using historical evidence effectively to support their positions. Their written arguments should reflect some in-depth grasp of issues and refer to both primary and secondary sources.[12]

Yet just 11 percent of high school seniors attained that level of

11. National Center for Education Statistics Web site, http://nces.ed.gov/nationsreportcard/civics/achieveall.asp.
12. See http://nces.ed.gov/nationsreportcard/ushistory/achieveall.asp.

mastery in 2001, whereas an alarming 57 percent scored below the "basic" level on that assessment.[13]

NAEP is not the only source of gloomy evidence that young people emerging from U.S. schools are cognitively ill-equipped for citizenship. There's less formal data about their preparation for such nonacademic dimensions as civic participation, being law-abiding, and community responsibility. But the available evidence is far from comforting when one looks at volunteering and voting rates among young Americans.

The Quest for Solutions

To what extent, if any, can government solve this problem? It has surely been trying, both on the curriculum side and by pushing for more "service learning" and suchlike. In his 2002 State of the Union message, President George W. Bush called for a new out-pouring of national service and voluntarism and announced cre-ation of a policy-coordination unit called the U.S.A. Freedom Corps.[14] He followed up in September 2002 with a stirring call for American schools to rededicate themselves to history and civics education and announced a multiagency effort to help make that

13. Twelfth-grade "basic" is described as follows (note that the 57 percent of high school seniors mentioned in the text were performing *below* this level on the 2001 National Assessment of U.S. history): "Twelfth-grade students perform-ing at the *Basic* level should be able to identify the significance of many people, places, events, dates, ideas, and documents in U.S. history. They should also recognize the importance of unity and diversity in the social and cultural history of the United States and have an awareness of America's changing relationships with the rest of the world. They should have a sense of continuity and change in history and be able to relate relevant experience from the past to their under-standing of contemporary issues. They should recognize that history is subject to interpretation and should understand the role of evidence in making an historical argument."

14. See *http://www.whitehouse.gov/news/releases/2002/01/20020129-11.html* for the president's text and *http://www.usafreedomcorps.gov* for information about the federal government's programmatic efforts in this regard.

happen.[15] His 2004 budget contains substantial sums to support essay contests, teacher training, and other elements of what the National Endowment for the Humanities calls its We the People program.[16] The Department of Education is home to another program, catalyzed by West Virginia Democrat Robert Byrd, who is widely known as the Senate's foremost history buff. Called Teaching of Traditional American History, it supports programs that seek to strengthen the knowledge base and pedagogical prowess of K–12 history teachers.[17] The Education Department also provides continuing support for worthy private programs and organizations, such as the Center for Civic Education.[18]

The Carnegie group and many others would have Washington expand its reach in civic education and spend a lot more money— even going so far as to urge the creation of a new federal agency to house and coordinate all such efforts. But are government programs and similar efforts to regulate, coerce, and "incentivize" schools the best or only way to tackle this problem? Perhaps not. A different approach would foster freedom, diversity, and competition in the field of education itself, notably by advancing the reform agenda that is usually termed "school choice," which accommodates the divergent views and priorities of ethnic and religious groups, parents, and educators in these domains, allowing them to tailor the approach they want for their children rather than settle for awkward efforts at a lowest-common-denominator political consensus for all public schools.

School choice takes many forms: publicly funded (and publicly accountable) "charter" schools; innumerable versions of public-school choice within and across district boundaries; magnet

15. See *http://www.usafreedomcorps.gov/about_usafc/whats_new/speeches/20 020917-1.asp* for the president's remarks.
16. See http://www.wethepeople.gov/.
17. See http://www.ed.gov/offices/OESE/reference/2c4.html.
18. See http://www.civiced.org/.

schools; home schooling; and attendance in privately operated
schools with a fiscal boost from vouchers, tax credits or scholar-
ships. The choice strategy received some encouragement in the
federal government's No Child Left Behind Act and is advanced
by the growth of charter-school programs in many states and
voucher programs in a few. But whereas similar choices are widespread at the preschool and postsecondary levels, they remain the
subject of intense controversy at the K–12 level. This controversy
stems from many sources and directions, but two of its recurrent
themes intersect with the subject of values and virtues.

First is the matter of state subsidy for instruction in religious
and parochial schools and the concern of some that this violates
the First Amendment's "establishment clause." (This debate no
longer arises when government assists college students to attend
Notre Dame or Yeshiva.) However, at least for the time being, this
issue has been laid to rest by the U.S. Supreme Court's decision in
the 2002 *Zelman* case,[19] which approved the publicly funded
voucher program that Ohio has been operating for low-income
children in Cleveland, notwithstanding the fact that most of the
voucher recipients attend Catholic schools. The Court said, in
effect, that this situation is permissible so long as the children's
choice of school is made by parents, not government.[20] This decision will ease "establishment clause" anxieties over school choice
as a matter of jurisprudence, but not as a matter of politics. Many
state constitutions contain their own prohibitions against public
dollars flowing into church-affiliated entities. These are often far

19. *Zelman v. Simmons-Harris*, 536 U.S. 639.
20. A major reason that such a large fraction of Cleveland voucher recipients
wound up in parochial schools is that suburban public schools refused to admit
them, even though they had this option under state law—and the Ohio program
is structured in such a way that the voucher amount is considerably larger when
redeemed in public schools. As low-income minority children living in inner
cities often discover, the prosperous suburban school systems across the munic-
ipal boundary want nothing to do with them.

more restrictive than even a Jeffersonian reading of the First Amendment and they were not undone by the Supreme Court's holding in *Zelman*. Moreover, watchdog groups continue to scan the education sky for any signs of slippage on the "establishment" front. It's more than a bit ironic, though, because in today's public schools pervasive secularism is a bigger problem from a values and virtues standpoint than is rampant sectarianism.

The second school-choice controversy that bears upon the present discussion is concern that the proliferation of distinctive schools, catering to different world-views, ethnic groups, social groups, or philosophies, will balkanize American society. Justice Breyer alluded to this fear in his dissent in the *Zelman* case, and it's not one to dismiss lightly, particularly by those who believe that schools could do better at forging citizens by imparting the "unum's" shared values to all young Americans. There is, however, evidence that private-school students are more civically engaged than their public-school classmates.[21] We have also seen that government-operated schools do a lackluster job in this area—and are so whipsawed by conflicting views that the chances of their doing much better seem remote. Moreover, so long as states retain the authority to establish core academic standards for all public schools and to mandate high-stakes tests keyed to those standards, they have the opportunity to mitigate the curricular balkanization, even in such fractious fields as social studies. In my view—admittedly a controversial one—it's reasonable for the state to insist that any child whose education is subsidized with public funds must acquire the knowledge and skills spelled out in the state's academic

21. David E. Campbell, "Bowling Together," *Education Next* (fall 2001). Available online at *http://www.educationnext.org/20013/55.html.* The unabridged version, complete with data, can be found at *http://www.educationnext.org/unabridged/20013/campbell.html.*

standards, even if that youngster attends a privately operated school.[22]

The Limits of Schooling

America has a considerable distance yet to traverse on the school-choice front even as we face a continuing problem on the virtues-and-values education front. In considering solutions to that problem, however, we do well not to focus obsessively on the schools. We must bear in mind that American youngsters spend relatively little of their lives there: only 9 percent of their hours on Earth between birth and their eighteenth birthdays.[23] This means that 91 percent of their time is spent elsewhere. School may, of course, influence a larger fraction of many days—if homework is intense, if extracurricular activities engage youngsters until late afternoon, if the school sponsors after-school projects and weekend events, and if the amount of time spent commuting to and from is large. The sense that life revolves around school is probably keenest in middle-class households where parents calibrate family rhythms to school schedules, oversee homework assignments, and limit television and other nonacademic pursuits lest they interfere with schoolwork. The picture is very different, however, for youngsters

22. This view is intensely controversial within America's private-school community, and for many schools such a requirement would be reason enough to eschew vouchers—and possibly even tax credits—and forgo the additional students.

23. One can easily calculate this. The numerator consists of 180 (the typical number of days in the school year, assuming perfect attendance) × 13 (the number of years of schooling from kindergarten through high school (assuming full-day kindergarten) × 6 (the number of hours in the typical school day, with no discount taken for recess, lunch, gym or study hall). The denominator is 365 (days in the year) × 18 (years on earth) × 24 (hours per day). The quotient is .09. If you want to allow for sleep, change the number of hours per day in the denominator to 16. Then the quotient is 13.3. But keep in mind that few youngsters have perfect attendance in school and that few schools devote a full six hours a day to academics.

from disorganized families and heedless parents, whose school attendance may be spotty, whose attention to homework may be rare, and whose lives from 2:30 p.m. until 8:30 a.m.—and all day on weekends and during the summer—are scarcely touched by the demands and expectations set by teachers and schools.

From a values standpoint, limited leverage on the school's part can be good or bad. On the positive side, it means that if parents, churches, and other nonschool institutions are purposeful and effective in their nurturing of youthful virtue, they can exert a powerful influence on how children will turn out. On the negative side, it means that, for many youngsters, time outside school is spent in the grip not of positive, value-shaping institutions but of the popular culture (or, worse, street and gang culture). In that case, even a conscientious effort by teachers and schools to instill sound values during their share of the day is apt to be swamped by the forces at work on youngsters during the other 91 percent.

The schools' modest leverage in children's lives poses an academic problem, too; youngsters simply don't spend enough time engaged in structured learning to end up learning enough. Certainly they don't spend as much time at it as do the children of many competitor nations. This problem is compounded when well-meaning people insist that schools also tackle sundry social problems by adding drug education, sex education, AIDS education, health education, and, indeed, character education, values education, or service learning, to their curricula. When those add-ons are squeezed into the same meager fraction of children's lives that the schools control, they are apt to push out some of the academic curriculum while probably also proving ineffective at solving the social problems to which they're addressed—the more so when, having entrusted these problems to the schools, other agencies and institutions and policies wash their hands of responsibility.

Against this backdrop, we find any number of contemporary

efforts to help schools do a better job on the values and virtues front. Some federal grant programs are designed solely for this purpose. There are special curricular materials, textbooks, teaching packages, even (lately) some cyberversions.[24] Experts such as Stanford's William Damon and organizations such as the Center for Civic Education are glad to supply guidance and instructional materials.[25] If one also considers the sizable public investment in such related domains as school-based programs for drug and violence prevention, one might even conclude that America is now making a substantial effort to enlist its schools as agents for developing sound values and behavior patterns in the young. Alas, one also has to say that the jury is out as to how well these special programs and extra services are working.

We must also ask how these special-emphasis programs compare in impact with the subliminal effects that schools and teachers have on children's values even when not meant to. The teacher is inherently and inevitably a role model, for good or ill. How she conducts herself, how she treats people, how conscientious she is, how well prepared—these are things that children notice, that they compare with other adults in their lives, and that they may pattern themselves after. The curriculum has a subliminal effect on values, too, particularly in literature and social studies. Which heroes (if any) are studied? Which villains? Or do curriculum and textbook settle for the softer values of being friendly, tolerant, and non-judgmental? Which works of literature are read, and on what basis are they selected? the author's race or gender? the timeless worth of the chosen works? Ravitch's research indicates that classic works

24. See, for example, the patriotism curriculum developed by K12, the private firm chaired by former Education Secretary William J. Bennett, which can be found at *http://patriot.k12.com/*. K12 also has a virtues program, to be accessed at http://www.products.k12.com/virtues/.

25. Much can be learned from *Bringing in a New Era in Character Education*, ed. William Damon (Stanford, CA: Hoover Institution Press, 2002).

of literature are being squeezed out of the K–12 classroom by overwrought anxiety about bias, noninclusiveness, political incorrectness, and so on. When, as often happens in the study of literature, the reader comes upon questions of human relations, morals, values, and ethics, how does the teacher explain them? What aspects are focused on? What lessons are learned?

The "extra-curriculum" matters, too. How the school functions and the sorts of activities it encourages help shape the nonacademic side of civic education. In "The Civic Mission of Schools," for example, the Carnegie group urges that students be enabled to participate in school governance and given many opportunities—even the obligation—to participate in service-learning programs outside the school itself.

Conclusion

Schools, in sum, are surely part of the problem and potentially part of the solution. Their inherent and subliminal influences may be more powerful than special add-on programs supplied by government and other outside forces. Ensuring that one's child is in the right school, with the right curriculum and the right teacher—this is important to the child's values as well as to his cognitive knowledge. I suspect it's more consequential than the presence or absence in his school of single-purpose efforts to impart values or develop character.

In the U.S. context, I believe, these salubrious circumstances are more readily obtainable within the framework of a liberal school-choice policy that encourages people to seek the best schools for their kids and does not get in the way of schools that are clear about their curriculum and choosy about their teachers (including those who never attended education schools) and that go out of their way to teach values, virtues, even religious faith. Such a regimen will strengthen the private side of the public-private balance that will surely continue to characterize K–12 education governance in America. As for the public side, it should focus on state efforts (with an occasional boost from Washington and, one hopes, conscientious implementation at the local level) to insist that all schools deliver a core curriculum that includes the essentials of history and civics. If that insistence also catalyzes a top-to-bottom overhaul of the subject known as social studies, everyone would benefit.

Marriage
and
Family

DOUGLAS W. KMIEC

Throughout the many perspectives in this volume is the seeming tension between the pursuit of virtue and freedom. Harvey Mansfield locates this tension in the philosophical principles embraced at the American founding. Stanley Kurtz posits that it is revealed to this day in the ongoing competition between the world-views of genuine religious faith that underlie the cardinal virtues of justice, temperance, fortitude, and prudence and the pseudofaith of individualism. David Davenport and Hanna Skandera find the ascent of individualism to be aided and abetted by thin forms of association that are bought and paid for with federal dollars. Chester Finn sees the nourishment of virtuous and competent character in education advanced by the individuality of school choice, but candidly admits that the path of choice over serious civic education entails its own risk of balkanization. We no longer come together to enliven and entertain the human spirit so much as to lobby as an NGO for specific political outcomes.

From the perspective of this chapter, none of this—how ever insightfully catalogued—should be surprising. Since the Genesis story, men and women have found the reconciliation of freedom and virtue to be difficult. This chapter finds the same to be true with respect to marriage and family. Families form because men and women are not intended to live alone. By nature, we are intended to live *in* society, not apart from it. The most basic society, the family, consists in husband and wife forming a marital union separate and distinct from their individual personalities. Millennia of religious instruction of every type and denomination holds out this marital union as an end in itself; as a positive, virtuous good. But how can that be when it requires the submission of individual freedom?

This chapter inquires into whether American marriage and the family built upon it—with or without the presence of children— is understood to be an end. Is it an end worthy of the seeming loss of individual liberty to pursue separate interests, ambitions, and pleasures in exchange for the wholeness and interconnected love of another? Or is marriage in twenty-first-century America merely a quaint formalism that is complacently indulged by individuals with little thought or expectation of its required mutual self-giving? And from the standpoint of the larger polity, if marriage is neither appreciated as an end nor consciously recognized and supported by law and public policy as an essential means of fostering its most important consequential good—the nurturing and formation of children—will it long survive?

Good questions. As elsewhere, the answers, I believe, will require us to navigate a religious perspective built on the paradox that we find individual freedom through obedience to our human natures. Less abstractly, that we find ourselves by freely giving ourselves to others. This generic religious principle has special relevance for marriage. But these religious sentiments are dimly heard because they are often weakly voiced in parish, church, or synagogue. Modern ears have a difficult time being told that we are to love, honor, and obey our spouses and that in those actions, we become more than we could ever hope to be alone. A world immersed in alluring electronic images of freedom through indulgence easily displaces the stuffy, Sabbath-day admonitions that we should submit to the truth of our natures in order to free them from addictions of self-centered lust or materialism or the trivial. The individualist vision will insist, of course, that we can have both freedom and commitment—though to most of us, it is never quite clear how. Instead, the path of individualism leads to half-formed marriages that are more contract than covenant; whose members in daily routine prefer work over family; and that because of their growing numbers even build entire neighborhoods and cities that are unmindful of the view of marriage as end or family as cultural educator.

As a matter of personal decision, which conception of marriage and family we affirm is indeed a matter of freedom. No religious view can or should be legislated. True faith depends on a change of heart, not the force of law, even as law and policy will inevitably be informed by faith of some sort. The limits of the law in the enactment of virtue and the prohibition of vice is conceded by even the most profound of moral philosophers, Thomas Aquinas. Tocqueville marveled in the early nineteenth century at how well Americans appreciated that the dogmatic beliefs of faith were far superior to the blunt edge of the law in the maintenance of virtue. Do Americans in the twenty-first century still agree, or is Stanley Kurtz right that progressive liberalism or individualism has become a pseudoreligion using the law to rule off-limits genuine religious perspectives?

This is not a chapter of despair, however, but of hope. So long as we hold fast to the notion that we are a nation that governs by consent, we make the law and can adopt the views we think fitting. If the public law of marriage and family is uncongenial to a full understanding of the importance of this institution, it is our own very solvable problem, no one else's. Indeed, given that it is still possible to see the family as its own legislator, at least for the small civilization within it, we need not wait for more favorable public law or policy in order to follow the path of virtue in our own lives.

After exploring how we understand marriage as either mutually covenantal or contractually individualist, this chapter identifies the cultural influences that pull us toward one view over the other. Along the way the chapter considers whether alternative legal or policy perspectives might more strongly support marriage and the families built upon it. The chapter concludes with a summary of these ideas.

Marriage As Mutual Covenant

The mutually covenantal conception of marriage is religious in origin. God is said to be the "author" of marriage, defining it as an indissoluble completion of two otherwise incomplete individuals. Indissolubility is conveyed in the language of covenant. Covenant is not mere promise. Neither is it legalistic. Thus, the covenantal idea of marriage stands in opposition to marriage in commercial or bargained-for terms as the exchange of consideration. In marriage, man and wife come to this covenant without their particular duties fully elaborated. Yet, duties do exist, though not found within a checklist or accomplished with the expectation of exact equivalent in return. The words "for better or for worse" are part of the common parlance of marriage, and they concisely and adequately express the Divine servanthood that marriage represents.

The covenantal view of marriage rejects the "what's in it for me" talk of contemporary culture. Thus, Linda J. Waite and Maggie Gallagher argue strongly against an individualized and privatized view of marriage. "[A]fter a decade of research, [they are convinced] that this . . . view of marriage is objectively wrong. Wrong in the sense that deep down, it is not the way, despite how we sometimes talk, most of us in America really look at marriage. And wrong in the sense that if we did adopt this view of marriage, marriage would lose its unique power. Agree to privatize marriage, in other words, and you do not expand people's choices—you effectively eliminate the choice to marry, for marriage means [raising] . . . your commitment to each other"[1] beyond the purely emotional, or as discussed below, the mundanely contractual.

Not surprisingly, the mutual covenant view of marriage has a unique understanding of sexual relations within marriage. Sexual intercourse is not just for individual pleasure, but it is "something fraught with emotional risks, fraught indeed with serious responsibilities. . . . [It] has [a] twofold natural purpose that must be respected—the purpose of bringing forth new lives and the purpose of uniting men and women together[.] [W]hoever participates in sexual activity must do so in a way that protects these natural goods. . . ."[2] The sexual relationship is an inclination toward the good, expanding the "opportunities for humans to love—not only to love one's sexual partner without qualification but also to love the offspring they may have. It allows spouses to build a family together and to have a meaningful life."[3]

Marriage: The Individualist or Consequentialist View

Modern American experience is, of course, not singularly religious. Because of this, there is less overt instruction on the reasons.

1. Linda J. Waite and Maggie Gallagher, *The Case for Marriage* (New York: Doubleday, 2000), 16–17.
2. Janet E. Smith, "Natural Law and Sexual Ethics," in *Common Truths: New Perspectives on Natural Law*, ed. Edward McLean (Wilmington, Del.: Intercollegiate Studies Institute, 2000), 205.
3. Ibid., 204.

According to census data, some 4 million Americans do not trouble themselves with discerning marriage's purpose at all, choosing simply to live together. Still, when a majority of Americans do reach a given age or stage of life experience, marriage remains culturally expected, even if it is tepidly welcomed with the uninformed shrug of "well, why not marry?" If the marital state is contemplated much beyond this in the competing secular or individualist view, marriage is a *means* to individual economic and social fulfillment, not a Divinely-ordained *end*. Seen as a means to individual fulfillment or status, it can, and given prevalent divorce rates, often is, set aside when the arrangement is found to be less than *individually* fulfilling. By design, therefore, a consequentialist, individualist conception of marriage is incapable of surpassing difficulty when life takes an unexpected turn not for better, but for worse.

Sexual intercourse within an individualist conception of marriage also differs markedly from the covenantal perspective. The individualist mentality, taking its cue from the media, emphasizes the physical, with little contemplation of the emotional or spiritual side of this physical unity. Yet, this separation of spirit from body is intellectually perilous because it allows the human body to be seen merely as "raw material" for the pleasure or satisfaction of others. Such separation is thus related to pornography (seeing the human body as object for pleasure, not as the sharing of a spiritually based sexual union in marriage), abortion (seeing the human body of the innocent child as an impediment to economic or social well-being), and cloning or fetal experimentation (seeing the human body of the unborn child as a resource for medical science). Similarly, Jennifer Morse observes: "It is easy to see how a woman in today's world could conclude that sexuality, intimacy, and childbearing could be and perhaps should be placed into distinct cubbyholes of one's life. We all received plenty of cultural messages telling us that sexual activity has no necessary connection with either procreation or deep personal intimacy. The organic connection that naturally exists between sex, procreation, and intimacy is almost hidden from public view and excluded from discourse."[4]

What cannot be hidden from view are the consequences of this course. The widespread availability and acceptance of contraceptive use did not reduce illegitimate births; it fomented it. "One might have thought that the increased availability of contraception would have offset the effects of increased sexual activity outside of marriage. But more children are born outside of marriage than ever before."[5] As Professor Janet Smith notes, this disconnect between law and morality does not seem to be working. Smith asks rhetorically: "What does the fact that 68 percent of African-American babies are born out of wedlock suggest? The figure is now 22 percent in the white community and rapidly growing. This figure, of course, would be higher if it were not for the one and a half million abortions a year. One of two marriages is going to end in divorce. AIDS is decimating some portions of our population. Are there any hints here that we are violating nature, acting irrationally, failing to live in accord with reality?"[6]

Marriage Conceptions and Family

Covenantal and individualist conceptions of marriage do not depend on the presence of children. Those seeing marriage as a mutual covenant of self-giving do have an easier time welcoming children, but even if a marriage is anchored in individualism, the physical and emotional needs of children have a way—sometimes a very insistent way—of getting us past self-interest. Once children

---

4. Jennifer Roback Morse, *Love and Economics—Why the Laissez-Faire Family Doesn't Work* (Dallas: Spence Pub. Co., 2001), 108.
5. Ibid., 111.
6. Smith, "Natural Law and Sexual Ethics," 203.

are present within a marriage, it is hard to understate the positive consequences for the larger society of committed marital partners serving as cultural educators. As one writer succinctly observed: "The loving family is surely the foundation of the moral and cultural leg of a free society, just as property rights and contract law are the foundations of the economic leg, and constitutionally limited government and freely elected rulers are of the political leg. . . . The moral and cultural tools of a free people include persuasion based upon reason and evidence, as well as the cultivation of appropriate 'habits of the heart' from birth to adulthood."[7] The point was seldom better put than the words of John Stuart Mill in his observation that "[t]o bring a child into existence without a fair prospect of being able, not only to provide food for its body, but instruction and training for its mind, is a moral crime."[8]

Given the importance of the family as cultural educator, many, like Janet Smith and Jennifer Morse, have pointed out troubling sociological data related to the instability of the individualist conception of marriage. "Data from the general social surveys indicate that 39 percent of all first marriages (which are more stable than remarriages) entered into during the 1970s . . . ended in divorce or separation before their fifteenth anniversary."[9] Indeed, in the last thirty years, America has witnessed a 400 percent increase in illegitimate births,[10] a quadrupling of the divorce rate,[11] and a tripling of the number of children living in single-parent house-

    7. Morse, *Love and Economics*, 229.
    8. John Stuart Mill, *On Liberty* (New York: Appleton-Century-Crofts, 1947).
    9. Morse, *Love and Economics*.
    10. In 1997, 32.4 percent of all births were to unwed mothers ("National Bureau of Vital Statistics Report," vol. 47 [April 29, 1999]).
    11. In 1970, 3.2 percent of the nation's population over age eighteen was divorced; by 1996, the percentage had increased to 9.4 percent (Statistical Abstract of the United States [1993] 53; [1997] 57).

holds.[12] The percentage of children living with both their biological parents was 70 percent in 1950, whereas in the 1990s, it was less than 50 percent.[13] Single parenting continues on the upsurge: increasing from 16 percent of all families to 18 percent just since 1990.[14] Most of these single-parent households are headed by women (41 percent).[15] And again, the number of Americans who live with someone of the opposite sex to whom they are not married has risen from 523,000 in 1970 to close to 4 million.[16]

Influences Affecting the View of Marriage

If a less covenantal, individualistic view of marriage can lessen the ill effects of the above statistics—be they school or societal violence, lesser educational achievement or poorer health[17]—what influ-

12. William J. Bennett, *The Index of Leading Cultural Indicators* (Washington, D.C.: Heritage Foundation, March 1993).

13. Richard Morin, "Unconventional Wisdom: New Facts and Hot Stats from the Social Sciences," *The Washington Post* (March 8, 1998), C5.

14. Barbara Vobejda, "Traditional Families Hold On; Statistics Show a Slackening of 1970s, '80s," *The Washington Post* (May 28, 1998), A2.

15. Ibid.

16. Thomas Hargrove and Guido H. Stempel III, "Poll Finds Most Would Marry Same Person Again," *Minneapolis Star-Tribune* (February 12, 1998), 14E.

17. The negative effects of divorce, including especially the negative effects on the children of divorce, have been studied comprehensively. See Barbara Dafoe Whitehead, *The Divorce Culture* (New York: Alfred A. Knopf, 1997); Paul Amata and Alan Booth, *A Generation At Risk: Growing Up in an Era of Family Upheaval* (Cambridge, Mass.: Harvard University Press, 1997); Mary Ann Glendon, *Divorce and Abortion in Western Law* (Cambridge, Mass.: Harvard University Press, 1987). Waite and Gallagher write: "Do we have any evidence that the divorce itself causes problems for children? The answer is simple: Yes, a great deal. In a snapshot, the risks of divorce and unwed childbearing look like this: Children raised in single-parent households are, on average, more likely to be poor, to have health problems and psychological disorders, to commit crimes and exhibit other conduct disorders, have somewhat poorer relationships with both family and peers, and as adults eventually get fewer years of education and enjoy less stable marriages and lower occupational statuses than children whose parents got and stayed married." Waite and Gallagher, *The Case for Marriage*, 125.

ences the culturally accepted view of marriage? There are many sources of influence—let's look at a few of them.

School Textbooks

School textbooks take a decidedly individualistic perspective. In the public school texts, for example, marriage is portrayed as "just one of many equally acceptable and equally productive adult relationships. These various relationships include cohabiting couples, divorced noncouples, stepfamilies, and gay and lesbian families."[18]

Sometimes textbook instruction is less cosmopolitan, choosing to see marriage as a patriarchal tool of oppression.[19] For example, Judy Root Aulette states that: "[m]arriage is an institution that exists in some societies but not in others and varies greatly from one society to the next, [but its essential purpose is] to control women and children."[20]

Other American textbook writers explicitly or implicitly mock the mutual self-giving the religious or covenantal perspective invites. To illustrate, John Scanzoni, in his *Contemporary Families and Relationships: Reinventing Responsibility*, posits that people in "fixed" (presumably, committed) marriages deprive themselves of necessary investments for self-fulfillment. As one reviewer put it, "a main goal of this book appears to be to persuade students not to be overly committed, not to love too much, and to be especially careful not to 'give' more than they 'get' in marriage and in other

---

18. Institute for American Values, *Closed Hearts, Closed Minds: The Textbook Story of Marriage*, ed. Norval Glenn (New York: Institute for American Values, 1997), 5.

19. Judy Root Aulette, *Changing Families* (Belmont, Calif.: Wadsworth, 1994).

20. Ibid., 273.

family relationships."[21] Of course, the idea of "loving [another] too much" is the antithesis of the religious understanding.

When the marital relationship is not caricatured, it is omitted from modern instructional tools dealing with sex, pregnancy, and child-rearing. As Linda Waite and Maggie Gallagher, in their groundbreaking work *The Case for Marriage*, observe, instructional texts on pregnancy and the like "[don't] even mention the word *marriage*. The closest reference to it is in the vague phrase: 'There are kids whose mothers and fathers live together.' A U.S. textbook salesman, explaining why *marriage* seldom appears anymore in the titles of college textbooks on marriage and the family said, the word sounds too 'old-fashioned' and 'preachy' to students."[22]

The Law of the Constitution

Another direct influence on how we understand marriage is the law. Given that the covenantal view of marriage is anchored in religious tradition, those that (mis)read constitutional history as mandating the separation of church and state, rather than freedom of religion,[23] heavy-handedly favor the individualist view by the expedient of making discussion of the religious or covenantal one difficult, if not impossible, in public instructional settings.

As a matter of original understanding, this favoritism of the individualist conception of marriage is certainly odd. The founders of the American republic premised our philosophical origin in the Declaration of Independence upon the "truth" that men and women are created by God and that natural rights, including the

21. Institute for American Values, *Closed Hearts, Closed Minds*, 8, discussing the Scanzoni text along with others.

22. Waite and Gallagher, *The Case for Marriage*, 8.

23. See Philip Hamburger, *The Separation of Church and State* (Cambridge, Mass.: Harvard University Press, 2003), documenting how the strict separationist idea was largely the product of anti-Catholic and anti-immigrant hatred of the nineteenth century, aided and abetted by the Ku Klux Klan.

natural right to marry, are part of an inalienable right to "pursue happiness." Not surprisingly, given this well-conceived beginning, state case law reflected, in appropriately nondenominational terms, religious values. Nowhere was this more apparent than in the laws pertaining to matrimony. The U.S. Supreme Court wrote in 1888 that marriage was far more than mere contract. "It is not so much the result of private agreement," said the Court, "as of public ordination.[24] In every enlightened government, [marriage] is preeminently the basis of civil institutions, and thus an object of the deepest public concern. In this light, marriage is more than a contract. It is not a mere matter of pecuniary consideration. It is a great public institution, giving character to our whole civil polity."[25]

Religion remains important to the individual American citizen, with more than 90 percent expressing a belief in God.[26] Nevertheless, the Supreme Court, especially in the period from 1960 to 1985, took some curious and religiously exclusionary turns. The high court's cases in this period exhibit the peculiar view that a nation founded on the belief in God could somehow maintain a legal system wherein the law must remain neutral between religion and irreligion. The acclaimed, historically and philosophically correct, view of freedom of religion became under these cases the flawed view of freedom *from* religion. One lower court, the Ninth Circuit, even proclaimed the pledge of allegiance, by virtue of its historically unassailable reference to "one nation under God," to

24. Notice the use of even religious terminology.

25. *Maynard v. Hill*, 125 U.S. 190, 213 (1888), referencing *Noel v. Ewing*, 9 Ind. 37, 50 (1857).

26. See generally Patrick Glynn, *God—The Evidence* (Rocklin, Calif.: Forum, 1997); see also Douglas W. Kmiec, *Cease-fire on the Family* (Notre Dame: Crisis Books, 1995) for an extended perspective on the relationship between marriage, family, and American culture.

be unconstitutional.[27] That the framers could easily reconcile a corporate or sovereign acknowledgment of transcendent authority (as both a source and security for unalienable liberty) with the Constitution's textual pledge of religious freedom seems to elude the appellate mind of some federal judges and many academics.

Not surprisingly, the Supreme Court's erroneous interpretations occurred at the zenith of the American cultural embrace of individual autonomy and challenge to civil institution generally. The 1960s and 1970s in America accepted notions of liberty without obligation that would have been rejected outright by those who guided America in its first century and a half. In approving access to artificial contraceptives by unmarried couples, the Supreme Court of the United States wrote: "the marital couple is not an independent entity with a mind and heart of its own, but an association of two individuals each with a separate intellectual and emotional makeup."[28] It is questionable how many individual Americans would describe their marriages in the same way, but it is evident that this undisturbed precedent remains the view of the highest court in the land and certainly has some influence on the perception of marriage as either mutual or individualistic.

The Law of the States—
Property Devices That Favor Individualism

At the state level, the American legal practice of prenuptial or premarital agreement reduces marriage to cost-benefit terms. Until 1970, prenuptial agreements in the United States were unenforceable if their intent was solely focused on the division of assets at the time of divorce. Prenuptial agreements were primarily intended to provide for the untimely death of a spouse. The judicial

27. *Newdow v. U.S. Congress*, 292 F.3d 597 (9th Cir. 2002), rehearing en banc denied, 321 F.3d 772 (9th Cir. 2003).
28. *Eisenstadt v. Baird*, 405 U.S. 438, 453 (1972).

rationale for voiding prenuptial accords prior to 1970 coincided reasonably well with the religious or mutual covenant perspective on marriage. Thus, it was not uncommon to find courts condemning such agreements because they were contrary "to the concept of marriage" or to marital "dignity and sacredness." In *Brooks v. Brooks*,[29] the Alaska Supreme Court summarized this earlier thinking: "[T]he traditional common law view was that prenuptial agreements in contemplation of divorce . . . were inconsistent with the sanctity of marriage and the state's interest in preserving marriage. . . . Courts uniformly viewed these agreements as inherently conducive to divorce and as allowing a husband to circumvent his legal duty to support his wife."[30]

In the last three decades, there has been a significant, and unfortunate, change of judicial course. In the Florida case of *Posner v. Posner*,[31] for example, the Florida Supreme Court opened the door for marriage to be treated like other forms of economic negotiation. Mocking the mystery of marriage, a court wrote: "[n]o longer will the courts in viewing antenuptial contracts invariably begin 'with the realization that between persons in the prematrimonial state there is a mystical, confidential relationship which anesthetizes the senses. . . .'"[32] After these decisions, "lawmakers in many states began making premarital agreements more readily enforceable. . . ."[33] Under the Uniform Premarital Agreements Act adopted in more than half of the states, neither nondisclosure nor unconscionability will void a prenuptial agreement.[34] It is fair to surmise that when everything from housework allocations to the number of children each spouse will accept becomes a matter for

29. 733 P. 2d 1044, 1048 (Alaska 1987).
30. Ibid., 1079.
31. 233 So. 2d 381 (Fla. 1970).
32. *Potter v. Collin*, 321 So. 2d 128, 132 (Fla. Dist. Ct. App. 1975).
33. Gail Frommer Brod, "Premarital Agreements and Gender Justice," *Yale L. J. & Feminism* 6 (1994), 229, 256–59.
34. 9B Uniform Laws Annotated 69 (1996) and Section 6.

advance negotiation (or subsequent litigation), mutual self-giving has taken second place.

Although prenuptial bargaining still occurs predominately among the affluent, a similar economic ethic has infiltrated the American common law, or default property devices, that affect the marital unit and lean it toward impermanence. Consider in this regard the community property system that dominates the heavily populated U.S. West. Nominally premised upon equality, the community property system supposes that all (or almost all) property acquired during marriage shall be owned not 100 percent by the marital unit, but 50/50 as distinct community shares that are capable of separate transfer, devise, and inheritance. The prescribed division thus keeps the "asset" bags of the spouses packed at all times.

There are property concepts that favor the mutuality of the marital unit. However, gaining acceptance for them is hindered by the historical mistreatment of married women in matters of property and civil rights, especially in English common law doctrines that were transplanted to America. In this context, responsible feminist literature in the United States does have historical truth on its side. That said, were the covenantal view of marriage to be favored, the closest property device to that conception would be the tenancy by the entirety, which in its strongest form precludes individual spouses from alienating marital property unilaterally and safeguards the marital home against the economic misadventures of husband or wife alone.[35] The tenancy by the entirety is little used, except in a handful of heartland states, such as Indiana. Instead, states have been mimicking the California experience by adopting community property–like principles derived from the

---

35. See *Sawada v. Endo*, 561 P.2d 1291 (Hawaii 1977), describing the tenancy by the entirety and its support of the family unit.

Uniform Marriage and Divorce Act of 1973. This has bad consequence. As an essayist has written poignantly:

> The modern efforts of married women [and I would add men] to remain pointedly independent, financially and intellectually and emotionally, from their partners, as a cushion against failure, are inimical to marriage. Either they "succeed" by preventing a genuine marriage from forming or they provoke a crisis fatal to the marriage. . . .
>
> To try to cheat the process, to try to hedge one's bets, is to deny the meaning of what one does on the wedding day. There must be a submission not perhaps of the will but of mere willfulness, a relegating of your obstreperous private preferences, not to second place behind your mate, but to second place behind the unity the two of you are achieving or have pledged to achieve.[36]

Work over Family

The American attitude of marital individualism, rather than the covenantal mutualism, is also present in the desire of both spouses to pursue market careers simultaneously, thereby creating increased tension in the performance of parenting and family duty. In 1999, the White House Council of Economic Advisors (CEA) released a report highlighting that American parents have twenty-two fewer hours each week to spend at home compared with the average in 1969.[37] According to the accompanying commentary, "U.S. workers now spend more time on the job than workers in any other developed country, creating a 'parenting deficit' which many fear may be related to youth problems of violence and sexual experimentation in even younger children."[38] The dramatic

36. Ellen Wilson Fielding, Common Wisdom, "Won't You Be My Valentine?" *Crisis* 43 (February 1991).

37. Council of Economic Advisors (CEA), "The Parenting Deficit," available online at *www.newecon.org/parentingdeficitcea-may99.html.*

38. Ibid., commentary by Brian Robertson.

increase is attributable mostly to the hours worked by better educated married mothers. Even more surprising, the rate of increase is higher for mothers with children under the age of five.[39]

Why is this occurring? It is apparently not wage-driven. The CEA report notes that over the thirty-year period of the study, wages were largely stagnant for college-educated men. They increased in nominal terms for married women. However, the report commentary notes that "in comparison to the sharp increases in working hours, [real] wage gains were extremely modest (only about 4%)."[40] One analyst opined: "Many parents could reasonably ask themselves whether a second income is worth the price of a drastically reduced amount of time available for their kids."[41]

That working more means less time for family is a most unhappy situation, yet Americans rarely permit themselves to see why. Long ago, Aristotle described work as properly directed to an end beyond itself; namely, toward leisure. Of course, by this, Aristotle did not mean endless hours at the shopping mall or the mindless watching of television sports channels. Instead, men and women were to pursue a form of leisure that invited the development of virtue, in themselves and others, and the performance of civic duty. That this is not contemporary reality is evidenced by the fact that many in the United States would have difficulty describing exactly what such noble aspirations mean. As David Davenport and Hanna Skandera point out in their chapter, the legal concept of association is a greatly underdeveloped one. Despite bemoaning the loss of intermediate or voluntary association activity, Robert Putnam continues to bowl alone.[42]

39. Ibid., part III.
40. Ibid.
41. Ibid.
42. Robert D. Putnam, *Bowling Alone* (New York: Simon and Schuster, 2000). Putnam was the first to identify the loss in modern America of active partici-

Of course, the possibility that work has become the modern form of association beyond marriage cannot be overlooked. Frances Olsen, a feminist thinker, helps us see how this might be when she bemoans the dualism that is thrust upon both men and women by having identity defined in one place [work] and personality in another [home].[43] Candidly, Olsen writes: "Antidiscrimination law does not end the actual subordination of women in the market but instead mainly benefits a small percentage of women who adopt 'male' roles."[44] Even more intriguing, Olsen observes:

> The dualism between life in the market and life in the family is [pronounced]. . . . We expect the market to achieve the efficient production of goods and services; it is not the arena in which we are supposed to develop our personalities or satisfy human relational wants. Pervasive hierarchy in the market is imposed and justified on grounds of efficiency. The market is the realm of alienated labor. The expression of the desires to develop personality and to interact with others is relegated to the family and simultaneously glorified and devalued. We see the market as a means to an end, whereas we see the family as an end in itself. The market is the arena for work and the production of goods; the family is the arena for most forms of play and consumption. Dividing life between market and family compartmentalizes human experience in a way that prevents us from realizing the range of choices actually available to us. Much of social and productive life seems effectively beyond our control.[45]

At the moment, men are still more likely to find happiness, or as Aristotle described it, a whole life well lived, because the dualism

---

pation in voluntary association and the yearning in modern Americans for community.

43. See Frances Olsen, "The Family and the Market: A Study of Ideology and Legal Reform," *Harv. L. Rev.* 96 (1983), 1497, 1571.

44. Ibid., 1552.

45. Ibid., 1564.

of market and family affects them less. The market readily gives men roles in which they can develop their individuality, use their intellect, and exercise authority. As a complement, home provides men an opportunity to express gentleness; to allow weakness and compassion to be uppermost—if only for brief periods in the evening. In love of wife and children, men thus gain some semblance of wholeness that the life of commerce denies them. But the situation for women is undeniably different. Whether by nature or biology,[46] it seems foolish to deny the fact that most women readily demonstrate talents that far exceed that of most men in sustaining the equilibrium of a home. For women, the resolution and smoothing of difficulty does indeed seem second nature. As Suzanna Sherry observed, "the cliché that women are more cooperative and less competitive than men may have some basis in fact."[47] Of course, it is true that women entering the marketplace "as employee or manager may more acceptably display traits that are considered masculine."[48] Yet, as Carolyn Graglia demonstrates, the entrance fee remains high because such entry seldom unites, or even harmonizes, the two worlds. Rather, it necessitates a sacrifice of one for the other, which, apparently, is seldom a choice fully wanted by either gender.[49]

46. Much literature supports nurture. In particular, the fact that ego development occurs at a young age and that girls are usually raised by someone of the same gender means that the inclination toward attachment is greater than that in males. See generally Nancy Chodorow, *The Reproduction of Mothering: Psychoanalysis and the Sociology of Gender* (Berkeley: University of California Press, 1978).

47. See Suzanna Sherry, "Civic Virtue and the Feminine Voice in Constitutional Adjudication," *Va. L. Rev.* 72 (1986), 543, 585.

48. See Olsen, "The Family and the Market," 1565.

49. Perhaps not surprisingly, this appears to be especially true of mothers because upward of 80 percent still state that they would prefer to stay at home with their own children if they could afford to do so. "Opinion Roundup," *Public Opinion*, July–August, 1988, page 36, found agreement with this sentiment from 88 percent of mothers surveyed in 1987. Indeed, a California poll of parents found 69 percent agreement with the statement "It is much better for a family

To avoid losing the personal fulfillment of either market or home, marital partners have turned to extended day care as a parental substitute. However, empirical research suggests that the quality of day care in the United States is quite low, with effects on child behavior and capability that are poor or adverse. As several researchers noted: "Minimally regulated private-child-care arrangements provide uneven and generally low-quality care. A research team for the National Institute of Child Health and Human Development recently estimated that only 11 percent of child care settings for children age three and younger meet standards for 'excellent' care. In part, quality is poor because the care is provided by a minimally educated and inadequately trained work force, some 22 percent to 34 percent of teachers in regulated child care centers and family child care settings do not have a high school diploma; . . ."[50] In addition, Dr. Nicholi of the Harvard Medical School testified before Congress that: "The studies confirm that child care relegated to agencies outside the home, regardless of the quality of the facilities and the training of the staff, can never substitute for the care of a parent who loves the child more than anything else on Earth."[51]

Dr. Nicholi has not been heard by the present generation of

---

if the father works outside the home and the mother takes care of the children." See Cathleen Decker, "Parents Tell of Decisions, Struggles in Child-Rearing," *Los Angeles Times* (June 13, 1999), A1, citing a *Los Angeles Times* poll. The same poll found 81 percent of mothers wished to stay home with their children, and affluent women (those with incomes above $60,000) were the ones most likely to say that children interfere with a career. A Public Agenda Poll from June 2000 found 62 percent of parents with children under the age of five preferring policies that would make it easier for one parent to stay at home during a child's initial years over improving child care. Of course, culturally, men are seldom asked the question directly as they should be.

50. Janet C. Gornick and Marcia K. Meyers, "Support for Working Families," *The American Prospect* 12 (January 2001), 6.

51. Armand M. Nicholi Jr., M.D., Harvard Medical School, hearing before the United States Senate, Subcommittee on Children and Families, "Caring for America's Children" (February 23, 1998).

working Americans or public or corporate decision makers. Indeed, the implications of vastly expanded substitute child care may be adverse not only for the child placed within that care, but also for the typically underpaid (and often foreign migrant) who acts as caregiver. Arlie Hochschild, a Berkeley sociologist, has dubbed this the "nanny chain," explaining how low-paid migrant workers typically leave their own children in the third world in dire poverty and without supervision. Not surprisingly, some of these children grow up with little or no cultural responsibility. Some, it might well be hypothesized, are snipers or terrorists in waiting. Hochschild writes: "Just as global capitalism helps create a third world supply of mothering, it creates a first world demand for it."[52]

As discussed next, even if the work-family balance could be seriously rethought, the place left abandoned by an ever-more demanding workplace—the family home and neighborhood—also needs redesign.

The Lost American Neighborhood

Another less obvious influence favoring the individualist conception of marriage is the physical environment in which we live. Modern land development in the United States runs against the interests of a fulfilled and connected family life. As one writer put it, "American communities are strikingly unfit for children."[53] It is that way by design. The organizing principle is exclusion and the segregation of uses, nominally for the protection of health and safety, but as it turns out, practically aggravating both. Residents

52. Arlie Russell Hochschild, "The Nanny Chain," *The American Prospect* 11 (January 3, 2000), 35.
53. David Popenoe, "The Roots of Declining Social Virtue: Family, Community, and the Need for a 'Natural Communities Policy,'" chap. 4 in *Seedbeds of Virtue*, ed. Mary Ann Glendon and David Blankenhorn (Lanham, Md.: Madison Books, 1995), 87.

are consigned by legally imposed planning and zoning requirements to live largely isolated lives in close proximity only to an
attached multicar garage.

Curiously, this American development pattern is marketed by
sales brochures inspiring thoughts of children playing in wide
yards, neighbors worshiping together nearby, grandparents close
at hand, and leisurely evening walks inviting pleasant conversation
with friends on their front walk or at a corner store. In other words,
the marketing tries to coincide with a covenantal understanding
of marriage that seemingly inspires both strong extended families
and civic association. The reality is often far different. The wide
yards are frequently empty because the children are in extended
day-care or after-school programs waiting for late-arriving and
exhausted parents to exit a clogged highway. By design, home and
office are kept in far distant "zones." Neighbors may worship, but
seldom nearby. Local churches, and the important spiritual and
charitable community-building they supply, are miles away, situ-
ated by regulatory edict along arterial roads.

No handy grandparents either. In-law or accessory dwellings
compatible with a fixed, retirement income are out of the question.
A leisurely walk is a possibility, but to where? Sidewalks, if they
exist, are narrow and treeless, circling cul-de-sacs. And heaven
forbid there should actually be a store down on the corner. The
American land-use planning and zoning model is one of strict use
segregation. In addition, the prevalence of divorce and the weakened interest in marriage has meant an increasing amount of
singles housing, or at best, houses for nuclear—not extended—
families in one place; businesses in another; stores in a third; and
churches still somewhere else. This creates a nice, neat, everything-
in-its-place appearance, but the design has serious problems.

For years, environmental engineers have recognized that this
type of land-use arrangement aggravates the problem of the automobile—most notably, air pollution. Urban planners estimate that

many households make up to 10 separate automobile trips a day. These excursions exact a heavy toll, not only on the family budget, but also on the sanity of mothers and fathers sentenced by an unsound physical layout to drive *everywhere*—school, store, church, library, park, office.

Even as 40 percent of working Americans will soon face making care arrangements for elderly family members, zoning laws keep Grandma and Grandpa—or even a newly married son or daughter struggling to get on their feet—from moving into an easily created "granny flat," or separate apartment on one's own property. The same restrictions evict benign computer and faxed-based home businesses. Convenience stores and retail shops, even those with well-appointed signage and façades, are unthinkable. Youngsters are thus deprived of the responsibility of doing family shopping and of the opportunity for an after-school or summer job.

This segregated land-use pattern still appeals to some, but there seems little reason to uniformly and complacently chisel it into local law. Private developers only make matters worse by adding the imposed microdetail of private restrictive covenants that control everything from house siding color to pet size. These specifications are touted as maintaining property values, and sometimes they do, but the cumulative effect of such public and private use restrictions is a sterile living environment that breeds juvenile boredom and separates, rather than unifies, families.

American architects are just beginning to realize the shortcomings of all this and that alternative—more marriage- and family-promotive—forms of development are possible. For example, the San Francisco–based Congress for the New Urbanism has advanced the methodology of neotraditional planning, promoting the construction, or reconstruction, of village centers.[54] Village

54. See the Congress for New Urbanism's Web site at www.cnu.org for a set of design principles as well as a bibliography of materials expanding these thoughts.

centers are what, years ago, we less elegantly called neighborhoods. Neighborhoods have a sense of place. Street patterns intersect and define it. There are walkable distances to the needs of daily life. Commercial uses are reasonably integrated with residential dwellings of all types. In short, the neotraditional prescription is a simple common sense one: neighborhoods require housing, schools, and parks to be placed within walking distance of shops, civic buildings, and jobs.

No physical environment is beyond redemption—not even so-called big-box retail outlets or discount stores. For example, accessory units and apartments can be inserted in, around, and sometimes even over such stores. Residential over retail was once commonplace in New York, Chicago, and other large cities. By reviving this pattern, architecturally undistinguished structures engulfed by dark, forbidding islands of asphalt can become inviting, attractive centers of activity. Parking is reoriented out back or on the street. Human needs are given preference over the automobile.

Neotraditional developments are now being planned or built across the country on a small scale. It remains to be seen whether these locations will have more than the look of community. They hold the promise of vibrant physical locations, but in order to flourish they need to consist of married couples who understand marriage as the foundation of community and not merely an economic convenience or a place to park the car when not at work.[55]

---

55. James S. Coleman, "Social Capital in the Creation of Human Capital," *American Journal of Sociology* 94 (1988), 95. The importance of establishing neighborhoods correlates with the late James Coleman's work on "social capital"—or the web of family networks that encourage as well as discipline or monitor children within it. Where families are strong and interconnected through local church or school, achievement soars, even when controlled for the socioeconomic status of the families.

Meeting the Challenges Ahead—
Possible Public and Private Policy Alternatives

Thus far we have examined the competing covenantal and individualistic conceptions of marriage and some of the influences that lead our cultural understanding in one direction or the other. As suggested throughout, not only has individualism obscured a full understanding of the spiritual side of marriage, but it also has yielded troubling divorce and illegitimacy rates and the numerous cultural dysfunctions that follow from this. Marriage and family relationships are intimate, and thankfully, outside the purview of most secular law. Although the legal and policy proposals that follow each have merit, they also readily reveal why the law, without personal commitment, is likely incapable of shoring up the mutual covenant understanding of marriage. That said, the most obvious step would be to make marital exit less commonplace.

Reforming No-Fault Divorce—
The Covenant Marriage Option

There is a nationwide movement in its infancy in America to reaffirm the importance of marriage by reforming divorce. State divorce laws were made uniformly "no fault" in the early 1970s. This effectively meant that either spouse could petition and obtain a divorce, even against the wishes of the other spouse, by pleading nominal "irreconcilable differences." Academic research confirms that divorce rates skyrocketed thereafter—in some places, by as much as 25 percent.[56] Reformers want divorce procedures to incorporate waiting or cooling-off periods at a minimum. But change does not come easy. A mandatory mediation measure died in May

---

56. Thomas B. Marvell, "Divorce Rates and Fault Requirement," *Law and Society Review* 23 (1989), 544.

1998 in Iowa, for example, and dozens of like-minded bills in thirty or more states have thus far gone nowhere.

The exception: voluntary covenant marriage, enacted first in Louisiana and Arizona. These states give couples a choice between: "well, I guess I do" and "I really do." A couple can choose the standard marriage, of course, but explaining such choice to one's true love is bound to be sticky. Covenant marriages, by contrast, require premarital counseling, an agreement to additional counseling if problems develop during the marriage, and a two-year waiting period before any divorce is granted, absent physical abuse, substance abuse, adultery, or abandonment.

It is entirely fitting that covenant marriage statutes have an exception for abusive relationships, but the exception should be realistically construed with a presumption in favor of preserving a marriage relationship. Were abuse to be liberally interpreted to include emotional distress, the exception would easily swallow the rule. Of course, some will argue that no distinction should be drawn and that a single mother in an emotionally troubled marriage ought to seek independence from her spouse. But as Jennifer Morse writes: "Granted, . . . the single mother is more independent of her child's father. But she is more dependent on the good graces of her employer, the competence of her child care provider, and the energy of her blood relatives."[57] Even worse than these heightened dependencies outside the family, which are far less stable than a marital partner,[58] is the greater likelihood of separation and divorce being followed by cohabitation and physical abuse. "According to a British study of child abuse, a cohabiting boyfriend

57. Morse, *Love and Economics*, 91.

58. After all, since the concept of family wage is not engrained in the market economy, an employer's interests are not in the support of the family, but on an employee's utility to the employer. Similarly, welfare, or governmental assistance, is governed by political choice, not the needs of mother and child. All of this is quite impersonal and, for that reason, a poor substitute for marriage and intact family.

is thirty-three times more likely to abuse a child than a married father who lives with the mother."[59]

Reviving Common Law Causes
of Action to Deter Divorce

Beyond covenant marriage, divorce might also be discouraged by making third parties liable in civil damages for actions that harm marriages. Under existing practice, criminal prosecution is seldom brought under fornication or adultery prohibitions, though these laws remain on the books in many states. When adultery leads to the break-up of a marriage, dissolution proceedings, including awards of maintenance and child support, can be thought to "punish" the wrongdoing spouse for illicit behavior. But what of the meretricious third party? The common law provided a civil action to a wronged husband whenever a third party intentionally enticed a wife to leave her home.[60] And in the late nineteenth century, the tort of alienation of affections was recognized: Facts demonstrated that the marriage was a happy one; that love and affection were destroyed; and that the wrongful or malicious acts of a third party resulted in the loss of love and affection.[61]

Is it far-fetched to reinvigorate such causes of action in the twenty-first century? Perhaps. Certainly, the abuses of the trial bar in other areas of litigation gives pause in itself. Nevertheless, if we are serious about conveying the cultural importance of marriage

59. Morse, *Love and Economics*, 92, citing Michael Gordon and Susan Creighton, "Natal and Non-natal Fathers as Sexual Abusers in the United Kingdom: A Comparative Analysis," *Journal of Marriage and the Family* 50 (February 1988), 99–105, and other works finding similar results in the United States.

60. See, for example, *Hyde v. Scyssor*, 79 Eng. Rep. 462 (1620); *Moullin v. Montleone*, 115 S. 447 (La. 1927).

61. *Heermance v. James*, 47 Barb. 120 (N.Y. App. Div. 1866); see also William Prosser and W. Page Keeton, *The Law of Torts*, 5th ed. (St. Paul, Minn.: West Publishing, 1984), Sec. 124, 929.

and family, perhaps it is not too much to ask that the destruction of a marriage by an intentional tort be put on par with other intentional injuries. As the North Carolina Assembly legislatively explained in contemplating updating this civil provision, "This tort is designed to protect marriages from third-party intrusion and to create accountability and penalties for third parties who pursue a relationship with a married person and alienate the affections of the married person from their spouse. Some argue that there is no way to measure how strong a deterrent this law is. . . . [However,] jury verdicts in favor of aggrieved spouses over the past several years have provided continued publicity and awareness of the law."[62]

Deterring Divorce by Putting Children First

Another legal step urged to discourage divorce is the "children first" principle. First articulated by Mary Ann Glendon of the Harvard Law School,[63] this principle would place the equivalent of a lien on all marital assets in favor of the maintenance and education of the children. The children's interests, in other words, have priority over any property claim or formal title of either spouse, or both of them, in a divorce. Professor Katherine Shaw Spaht has proposed model legislation based on this principle, the Family As Community Act, which would apply existing property concepts and intestate distribution to recognize in the children of a marriage an "inchoate right in property acquired at any time during the marriage which matures into a legal interest at divorce.

---

62. John Rustin and Jere Z. Royall, "Protecting Marriage," North Carolina Family Council Pamphlet (June 2002).

63. See, for example, Mary Ann Glendon, *New Family, New Property* (1981), and "Fixed Rules and Discretion in Contemporary Family Law and Succession Law," *Tulane Law Review* 60 (1986), 1165.

. . ."[64] Thus, any thing—houses, cars, clothing, artwork, bank accounts—acquired during marriage (regardless of how titled) is "family property." Upon divorce, family property is applied first to meet parental obligations, such as education, and any net property residual is then equally divided among all family members. Portions given to the children are held in trust and effectively managed by the "residential," or custodial, parent.

Like any legal solution to a social problem, the remedy is surely incomplete and insufficient to rectify fully the harm of divorce. Nevertheless, Professor Spaht is correct that "the fulfillment of parental obligations [under the proposed model] may [fairly] be characterized as an award of divorce compensation. That is, given the volume of information concerning the negative effects of divorce on children, this award could attempt to compensate for (uncompensable) damage done to the child by the divorce."[65]

More Effective and Comprehensive
Premarital Counseling and Materials

This discussion of divorce deterrence should not obscure the positive steps that can be taken to strengthen the marriage bond and the family—for example, increased emphasis upon marital preparation. Canon 1063 in the Catholic tradition obligates pastors to provide "personal preparation for entering marriage so that through these means the Christian faithful may be instructed concerning the meaning of Christian marriage and the duty of Christian spouses and parents."[66] Similarly, Pepperdine University in California, an interdenominational Christian school affiliated with

64. The concept also applies at death of a spouse. See Professor Spaht's proposed model Family As Community Act on the Communitarian Network's Web site at www.gwu.edu/~ccps/.

65. Ibid., n. 59 within Professor Spaht's article.

66. Bernard A. Siegle, *Marriage: According to the New Code of Canon Law* (New York: Alba House, 1986), 27, citing and discussing the code.

the Church of Christ, has been a leader in marriage preparation and sustenance, through its Marriage and Family Institute. Michael McManus, a religious and ethics writer, has spearheaded a campaign, called Marriage Savers, that has drastically reduced the divorce rate in dozens of cities. Finally, Dr. James Dobson, an evangelical Protestant counselor who has a nationwide radio audience , heads a pro-marriage, pro-family organization called Focus on the Family, based in Colorado.

Since 1982, there has been a fourfold increase in the number of couples receiving marriage preparation.[67] These counseling sessions frequently involve religious leaders and mentor couples as well as a testing or inventory of the couple's personal dispositions to identify possible areas of conflict. Places where programs like Marriage Savers or the Catholic equivalent, Retrouville, exist have had divorce rates well below the national average. For example, in one of the counseling sites, Modesto, California, during a period when the national divorce rate was fairly stable or falling only slightly, the divorce rate plummeted locally by 35 percent.[68] The counseling efforts seem to have most effect on two of the most troubling predictors of divorce, namely youth (getting married under the age of 20) and cohabitation. Counselors make good use of a University of Wisconsin study that found couples who lived together before marriage have an 85 percent failure rate. As one counselor tells his couples, "Living together is the absolute worst thing you can do if your goal is a successful marriage."[69]

67. James A. Fussell, "Great Expectations, Surprise Revelations—More Couples Are Turning to Premarital Counseling," *The Kansas City Star* (May 31, 1998), H1.
68. Ibid.
69. Ibid.

Grasping the Significance of Marriage and the Family's Moral Responsibilities

A family is often referenced as "the first vital cell of civilization." Quite literally, the family structure introduces us to one another. As one author put it well: "Traditional society is composed of only two kinds of people—relatives and strangers. The social world centers around kinship identities, and relatives are those with whom you work, worship, ally, sleep, play, and die. Kinsmen bear you, nurse you in illness, initiate you into adulthood, protect you from injustice, and bury you into the order of the ancestors."[70] Looking at that list, it is quickly evident that in traditional society every critical activity in life is performed with, through, or for the family. Things are different today, but the family still needs to perform care functions.

As noted, a religious or covenantal understanding of marriage is built upon the giving of the total self. Nurturing this conception is vital if the American family is to meet internal and external expectations. Inside the family, we envision the family as a source of "love and emotional support, respect for others, and taking responsibility for actions."[71] Behind the description of love or caring is the idea of constancy, family ritual. In other words, true emotional support is thought to be derived from being together for both important and unimportant times. The notion of "quality time," fashionable in American family literature in the 1980s to rationalize husband's *and* wife's preference for work over family, is fraudulent.

---

70. David W. Murray, "Poor Suffering Bastards," *Policy Review* 73 (spring 1994), 74.

71. Mark Mellman, Edward Lazarus, and Allan Rivlin, "Family Time, Family Values," in *Rebuilding the Nest*, ed. David Blankenhorn, Steven Bayne, Jean Bethke Elshtain (Milwaukee, Wisc.: Family Service America, 1990), 73.

Outside the family, our expectation is that parents instill "respect for others," underscoring the importance of the pursuit of virtue that can only meaningfully begin within a family. Perhaps, today, the terminology of prudence, fortitude, temperance, and justice is not as well-known to American families as it should be, but there is a clear expectation that families build respect for people in authority, between parent and child, and for others generally. Despite an ever-greater off-loading of responsibility upon teachers, the community still largely expects families to form the moral character of their children. The consequence of failing in these tasks is reflected in troubling increases in violent crime and declines in educational achievement and general levels of civility. One family researcher describes what is being lost as the family's unique capability "of keeping alive that combination of obligation and duty, freedom and dissent, that is the heart of democratic life."[72]

Society also counts on families to produce a level of personal contentment necessary for social order. Happiness is something of an art. It requires a willingness to live in the present, rather than to worry over the past or the future. Families are the best source of this perspective because both spouses and children emphasize the element of *now* to a larger degree than does business, government, and investment activity.[73] "While differing on many things,

72. Jean Bethke Elshtain, "The Family and Civic Life," in *Rebuilding the Nest*, 128.

73. At the World Family Policy Forum in January 1999, Dr. Alan Carlson made note of the following: (1) A seventeen-nation study of marital status and happiness, showing "perhaps the most sweeping and strongest evidence to date in support of the relationship between marital status and happiness." The results, reported in the summer 1998 issue of the *Journal of Marriage and Family*, are consistent across countries and equally positive for both genders. (2) By contrast, single-mother households "experience an 85 percent increased risk of dying of heart disease" according to the *Journal of Health and Social Behavior* (1998). (3) Same-sex partners have a greater risk of violence at the hands of a partner by a multiple of four. On the web, Dr. Carlson's paper can be located at *www.fww.org/articles/wfpformum/acarlson.htm*. Waite and Gallagher, in *The Case for Marriage*, 67, similarly conclude that "married men and women report less depression, less

the great faiths show that the deepest meanings and the greatest satisfactions for humankind are to be found in family living."[74]

A Family Wage

To ameliorate the work-family "time crunch" and counter the overreliance upon day care, some have proposed a variant of the family wage. This idea, once championed by the Catholic Church, argues that there is a corporate social responsibility to provide a wage sufficient for an employee to sustain his or her children and a stay-at-home spouse. The idea of an imposed wage cuts against the grain of market reality, but enhanced family allowances to permit one of the spouses to reduce hours worked or child tax deductions[75] might be alternative approaches for capturing the desire to have a better work-family balance while respecting the fact that often women and men alike desire the fulfillment of both home and workplace.

Conclusion

Americans are united in anxiety since 9/11. Yet, if these basic security concerns could somehow be set aside, the prevalent American culture would remain highly individualistic even as there are

anxiety, and lower levels of other types of psychological distress than do those who are single, divorced, or widowed. . . . When it comes to happiness, the married have a similarly powerful advantage. One survey of 14,000 adults over a ten-year period, for example, found that marital status was one of the most important predictors of happiness."

74. Waite and Gallagher, *The Case for Marriage*, 5.

75. A Public Agenda online poll in June 2000 found that 64 percent of parents with children under age five would support giving "a much bigger tax break to parents who stay at home to care for their children. This was the preferred policy, over requiring employers to give paid parental leave, which is now law in California, increasing funds for Head Start, or extensions of after-school programs. Public Agenda describes itself as a "nonpartisan, nonprofit public opinion research and citizen education organization," founded in 1975 by social scientist Daniel Yankelovich and former Secretary of State Cyrus Vance.

provocative academic conferences on communitarianism and a subtle yearning for authentic community in the larger population.[76] One empirical Communitarian Network study found that when "asked specifically about the role of the government in legislative changes that might affect the rate of divorce, respondents overwhelmingly supported the individualist position of leaving it to the couple themselves to decide. . . . [T]here is still significant support for the individualist position. Respondents tended toward nonintervention, at least in matters that affect them directly."[77] As another writer puts it: "The goal seems to be to find the minimal set of human relationships that a child can have and still turn out tolerably well. . . . People from across the political spectrum seem to be saying, 'What do I have to do in order to maintain my position that divorce or single parenthood is not harmful to children? How much money does society have to spend to make up for the loss of the relationship so that I will not have to give up my belief that parents are entitled to any lifestyle choices they want?'"[78]

We thus persist in going our separate ways as spouses. And in the face of this, policy proposal after policy proposal unrealistically asks stepfathers and cohabiting boyfriends or same-sex partners to behave like biological fathers or mothers. Others demand the law to crack down on "deadbeat dads." No one has a brief for any parent forfeiting responsibility, but how realistic is it "to expect that a father who has been expelled from his home in a nasty divorce will contribute the same amount of money that he would if he were part of a functioning family"?[79] Yes, divorce laws can be reformed to make separation more difficult or, in the event of divorce, to put the children's economic interests first, but the law

76. See David Karp, "Americans as Communitarians: An Empirical Study," *The Responsive Community* 7 (winter 1996–97), 42.

77. Ibid., 46.

78. Morse, *Love and Economics*, 102–103.

79. Ibid.

cannot substitute for the emotional loss and the loss of support that the dissolution not just of a marriage, but of a family entails. The law in a free society cannot prevent bad choices without denying freedom, but it can force us to think clearly and to address the consequences of our errant choices when we make them.

It is time for red herrings to be discarded. Parents' interests in lifelong happiness and children's in emotional stability and direction actually coincide. Neither interest is advanced by a ready embrace of autonomy—the doctrine that each individual is his own law—either in the preference of work over family or divorce over marriage. Thinking otherwise is *learned* behavior. It can be *unlearned*. To summarize some of the public and private policies that could advance this reeducation in favor of marriage and family:

1. Encourage religious leaders and communities to more overtly and consistently articulate the cultural value of a covenantal over individualistic view of marriage.

2. Apply this covenantal view of marriage to the evaluation of the suitability of textbooks in educational settings.

3. Encourage states, through model legislation and amicus intervention before state common law courts, to revive or perpetuate forms of marital property ownership that do not keep "marital bags" packed and facilitate divorce—for example, preferring the tenancy by entirety over community property.

4. Attribute greater value to time with family by reducing the number of hours worked in marketplace activity. Explore cultural or policy means for instructing that "work is for man; man is not for work." At the same, time acknowledge that home and work facilitate the development of the whole human personality.

   a. Promote and defend the legality of gender-neutral compensation schedules that supply workplace bonuses for head of household responsibility; relatedly, favor enhancement of child allowances under the tax code.[80]

   b. Be skeptical of third-party child care, recognizing it for what it is—a lesser quality substitute for family-provided care and instruction.

   c. Mitigate land-use segregation, which compounds the difficulty of striking a reasonable work-family balance and prevents the formation of genuine neighborhood or community.

5. Forthrightly question sexual license. In particular, work against legal or cultural acceptance, if not affirmation, of cohabiting or nonmarital relationships. "Cohabitation is not just like marriage. On average, cohabiting couples are less sexually faithful, lead less settled lives, are less likely to have children, are more likely to be violent, make less money, and are less happy—and less committed—than married couples."[81]

6. Enhance strong marital formation and commitment through the enactment of covenant marriage laws as well as the encouragement of religious consortiums that premise marital rites upon adequate instruction.[82]

---

80. Dependent allowances for children should more accurately reflect the true out-of-pocket cost of raising a child and should reflect the value of a parent at home providing care. In short, the tax code needs to be oriented toward the family. Ironically, the recent reform to eliminate the so-called marriage penalty, in fact, encourages both spouses to prefer market compensation over family responsibility. C. Eugene Steurele, "The Effects of Tax and Welfare Policies on Family Formation," in *Strategies for Strengthening Marriage: What Do We Know? What Do We Need to Know?* (Washington, D.C.: Family Impact Seminar, 1998), 153–62.

81. Waite and Gallagher, *The Case for Marriage*, 201.

82. "In 1998, Florida passed the Marriage Preparation and Preservation Act. Under the Florida law, engaged couples who complete a marriage-preparation course pay reduced marriage-license fees" (Waite and Gallagher, *The Case for Marriage*, 197). A small incentive, to be sure, but one that substantively makes

7. Repeal no-fault divorce, substituting a model that precludes divorce until after a significant waiting period of one year or more after applying for divorce,[83] and the completion of marital dispute resolution through either public or faith-based organizations.

8. Deter divorce through the revival or maintenance of common-law actions for "alienation of affection" against third parties who, under present law, bear little, if any, damage liability for the break-up of a marital union. Relatedly, factor fault into marital property division to increase the disincentive against infidelity.[84]

9. In the event divorce is unavoidable, preclude any division of marital property between the divorcing spouses until after the adequate vesting of property in the children to secure education and care needs.

10. Recognize that public policy and legal refinement is always secondary to personal commitment.

The unlearning of anti-marriage attitudes and the avoidance

---

an important statement and that invites religious communities to be more active and explicit instructors as well. Indeed, the private effectiveness of such instruction begs scholarly examination because more than 80 municipalities now have community marriage policies that involve the taking of marital inventories and meetings with trained mentoring couples (198).

83. "Before no-fault, waiting periods of two or three years were common in the United States and five-to-seven-year waiting periods were typical in Europe. . . . [Today,] [m]ost states have no waiting period at all" (Waite and Gallagher, *The Case for Marriage*, 196).

84. Milton C. Regan Jr., "Postmodern Family Law: Toward a New Model of Status," in *Promises to Keep: Decline and Renewal of Marriage in America*, ed. David Popenoe, Jean Bethke Elshtain, and David Blankenhorn (Lanham, Md.: Rowman & Littlefield, 1996), 157–85.

of culturally destructive behavior best occurs one family at a time.[85] And when it does, "[w]hen people are able to discover that the intertwining of [marital sex, procreation, and intimacy] deepens and enriches every aspect of their lives [and anchors the cultural instruction upon a stable family], it is as though they have stumbled onto a great secret unknown to any other member of the human race."[86]

Indeed, understanding the subtle and important relationship between marriage and family is a tremendous revelation, but no culture that wants to prosper morally or economically can long keep the benefits of marriage and family a secret.[87] Each generation depends on the one previous to identify that which must be treasured in life. Show me the objects that the people love, said Saint Augustine, and I will tell you their character.

85. This was the premise of my book, *Cease-fire on the Family* (1995), in which I argued individual families are fully capable of overcoming cultural dsyfunction or antagonism. The aspiration of purpose I held out for the family included: conquering the isolation and anonymity of a life alone; welcoming children out of a loving desire to cooperate with God's creative plan; nurturing the physical, intellectual, moral, and spiritual formation of children, unashamedly and clearly transferring to them the mega-virtues of belief in God and a knowable truth and the personal, cardinal virtues of prudence, fortitude, temperance, and justice; understanding that schools are extensions of responsible parenting, not replacements for it; encouraging the continued presence of an extended family in the lives of children, as in family elders connecting the past with the present; making one's family a part of a network of families united by faith, active in church, and open to its moral instruction; and uniting one's family with other families joined by a sense of place and local community.

86. Morse, *Love and Economics*, 108.

87. Waite and Gallagher (*The Case for Marriage*) write: "We need to place marriage in a prominent place on the public agenda. We need to discuss the foundational importance of marriage to family life, its importance to society as a whole, and its importance to individuals" (188).

Contributors

Peter Berkowitz teaches at George Mason University School of Law and is a research fellow at Stanford's Hoover Institution. The author of *Nietzsche: The Ethics of an Immoralist* (1995) and *Virtue and the Making of Modern Liberalism* (1999), he also is a contributing editor at *The New Republic* and writes on ethics, law, and politics for a wide variety of publications. He serves as a senior consultant to the President's Council on Bioethics.

David Davenport is a research fellow at the Hoover Institution and is distinguished professor of public policy and law at Pepperdine University. He served as president of Pepperdine University from 1985 through 2000.

Chester E. Finn Jr. is a senior fellow at Stanford's Hoover Institution, president of the Thomas B. Fordham Foundation and Thomas B. Fordham Institute, and senior editor of *Education Next*. His primary focus is the reform of primary and secondary schooling. Finn is also a fellow of the International Academy of Education and an adjunct fellow at the Hudson Institute, where he worked from 1995 through 1998.

Douglas W. Kmiec holds the Caruso Family Chair in Constitutional Law at Pepperdine University in California. A well-known commentator in the national media on constitutional subjects, he has authored numerous books and articles, including *The American Constitutional Order* (1999), now going into its second edition. Professor Kmiec has served as dean of the Catholic University of America Law School, taught for nearly two decades at Notre Dame Law, and served Presidents Ronald Reagan and George H. W. Bush as constitutional legal counsel.

Stanley Kurtz is a research fellow at Stanford University's Hoover Institution. He has a doctorate in social anthropology from Harvard University and has taught social theory and cross-cultural psychology at Harvard University and the University of Chicago.

Harvey C. Mansfield, the William R. Kenan Jr. Professor of Government at Harvard University, studies and teaches political philosophy. He has written on Edmund Burke and the nature of political parties, on Machiavelli and the invention of indirect government, in defense of a defensible liberalism, and in favor of a constitutional American political science. He has also written on the discovery and development of the theory of executive power and is a translator of Machiavelli and Tocqueville. He held Guggenheim and NEH fellowships and was on the Advisory Council of the NEH.

Hanna Skandera is a research fellow at the Hoover Institution. Skandera specializes in K–12 education policy and the intersection of American culture and values. She recently co-authored the book *School Figures: A Look at the Details behind the Debate* (2003) and is an adjunct professor at Pepperdine University's School of Public Policy.

Index